HOW TO BECOME

FILTHY, STINKING RICH THROUGH NETWORK MARKETING

D1111884

HOW TO BECOME

FILTHY, STINKING RICH THROUGH NETWORK MARKETING

WITHOUT ALIENATING FRIENDS AND FAMILY

MARK YARNELL · VALERIE BATES
DEREK HALL · SHELBY HALL

WILEY

John Wiley & Sons, Inc.

Published by John Wiley & Sons, Inc., Hoboken, New Jersey.
Published simultaneously in Canada.

For general information on our other products and services or for technical support, please contact our Customer Care Department within the United States at (800) 762–2974, outside the United States at (317) 572–3993 or fax (317) 572–4002.

Wiley publishes in a variety of print and electronic formats and by print-on-demand. Some material included with standard print versions of this book may not be included in e-books or in print-on-demand. If this book refers to media such as a CD or DVD that is not included in the version you purchased, you may download this material at http://booksupport.wiley.com. For more information about Wiley products, visit www.wiley.com.

Library of Congress Cataloging-in-Publication Data:

How to become filthy, stinking rich through network marketing: without alienating friends and family/ Mark Yarnell . . . [et al.].
      p.   cm.
Includes index.
ISBN 978-1-118-14426-8 (pbk); ISBN 978-1-118-22572-1 (ebk); ISBN 978-1-118-23307-8 (ebk); ISBN 978-1-118-26370-9 (ebk)
      1. Multilevel marketing. I. Yarnell, Mark, 1950-
HF5415.126.Y366   2012
658.8'72—dc23

2011044317

Printed in the United States of America

10 9 8 7 6 5 4 3

This book is dedicated to a better future for our precious children and grandchildren: Amy, Eric, Christine, Kennedy, and future generations.

—Mark and Valerie

We dedicate this book to our four grown children, Bradley, Trevor, Allison, and Amanda, and their spouses, as well as each of our 18 grandchildren. The roles you play in our lives add meaning to each and every day.

—Shelby and Derek

CONTENTS

ACKNOWLEDGMENTS

We acknowledge those individuals we admire as business experts and pioneers, whom we have mentioned throughout this book, namely: Dr. Taylor Hartman, Robert K. Greenleaf, Larry Spears, Alfred Alder, Warren Buffet, Sam Walton, Harland Sanders, Larry H. Miller, Dave Thomas, and Henry Ford. We also thank professional network marketers and personal friends, Jerry Campisi, Albert Muir, A. J. Monte, Marshall Douglas, and Judge Vernon Douglas.

A special acknowledgment to Vincent Hall, patriarch to a new generation of American citizens, who, as a coal miner in Yorkshire, England, had the vision for a better life at age 34 to uproot his wife and four children and emigrate to America, seeking the opportunities only this great country can provide.

— Derek and Shelby Hall

Heartfelt thanks to those professional networkers whose leadership continues to inspire so many to follow their own path to freedom, fulfillment, and legacy and whose stories we have told here: Margie Aliprandi, John Terhune, Debbie Campisi, Donnie and Dianne Walker, Danelle Rich, Laura Kall, Donna Imson, and Amber and Dean De Grasse.

We're so grateful to our talented daughter Christine Perkio for her many years of outstanding support in our writing and networking endeavors.

— Valerie Bates and Mark Yarnell

INTRODUCTION

Mark Yarnell

Thanks to the field of network marketing, I have lived a charmed life. It didn't start out this way, though; like most of my baby boomer peers, I blindly accepted and lived according to a significant lie until I was 36 years old: I believed that I had to choose between quantity of stuff or quality of life. In essence, I either had to give up precious time with those I loved, or I needed to accept a less demanding career with minimal rewards in exchange for enhanced personal freedom. I took a shot at both scenarios, and neither brought fulfillment.

When I succeeded financially in my early twenties, by working 60-hour weeks, I desperately longed for more time to enjoy my family. After changing careers and shifting my focus from the automobile industry to the ministry, I found myself with plenty of time but limited income. Had network marketing never surfaced, I'm sure, like most of my friends, I would have gone to my grave believing the lie. But for the past 25 years, I've been able to enjoy wealth and time-freedom—compliments of network marketing.

As luck would have it, a close friend and church member approached me in April of 1986 with a ground-floor network marketing opportunity at precisely the time that my banker was threatening to repossess my used car. With no college degree to fall back on and limited time to solve my debt crisis, I decided to give this industry a shot. It was a serious gamble; I had to borrow some capital just to pay bills, and the last thing I needed was to incur more debt by investing in my own business. But I took the risk and, as the saying goes, the rest is history. Within a year I was earning

10 times more money than I had ever earned in any of my previous positions—and I had all the free time I needed to relocate to Aspen, Colorado, where I could snow ski and hang glide to my heart's content.

Network marketing was the vehicle by which I was able to achieve freedom in the arenas of both personal wealth and personal time. The first year was a whirlwind of self-indulgence, during which I centered my life on extreme sports and expensive toys. However, I began to feel worthless toward the end of that year. There was a huge gaping hole that I couldn't seem to plug with material possessions, and I felt like I was squandering my free time. That's when I decided to go back to work.

Since my work focused on building my network marketing organization, I contacted the home office to find out where the smallest number of distributors were located. It turned out to be Jacksonville, Florida, so I relocated there and spent a year recruiting new people.

I moved many times over the next several years, and both my income and my free time continued to increase. In hindsight, I was probably looking for a geographical cure to boredom—which I never found. But along the way I began to write magazine articles about network marketing, and in 1996 a major publisher asked me to write a book about our industry.

Little did I know at the time that the book—which I called *Your First Year in Network Marketing*—would become an international best seller. But it did; and as a result, I became well known in many countries. Few authors are blessed to publish a book that enjoys a shelf life of more than a few months, and those of us who manage to write one soon realize an interesting fact: Ideas, like technology, ultimately become obsolete. I am proud of and thankful for my many readers, but I wrote that book before anyone had ever constructed a website, sent a text message, or received an e-mail. I wrote it before the technology bubble burst during the pre-9/11 halcyon days, when network marketing was a different animal.

For that reason, I and my coauthors have written this book, which is about network marketing in a new and radically different millennium. With thousands of companies from which to choose, and millions of people caught in the financial meltdown, there has never been a time when clarity and due diligence were more necessary. There are a number of questions that must be addressed, and we intend to tackle them in the following pages.

Let's begin with some very provocative ones: What are your financial options? If not through network marketing, how do you intend to generate enough capital to live well and retire comfortably? What are you planning to do about any current debt you have? Are you satisfied with the amount of taxes you pay? How do you feel about the fact that many of those tax dollars are being used to pay huge bonuses to corporate leaders in the financial sector because the government has decided that some companies are "too big to fail?" What would happen if gas prices go up to $10 per gallon? Could you survive for a couple of years without working, in the event of an unexpected accident or illness?

Let's follow those with more topic-specific critical questions: If you were to discover that this sector is far safer than Wall Street, real estate, or day trading, would you have any idea how to select a legitimate network marketing company? Do you know the difference between a pyramid scheme and a legal direct selling company? Do you know how much capital a company needs to expand internationally? Are you better off getting involved with a publicly traded networking company or a private one? Do you know the tax advantages of owning a home business—and if not, who will teach you? How important to your success is the upline sponsor who is the person above you on the team who enrolls you in the business, and what do you do if he or she is a novice networker? How do you find prospects when you run out of friends and family—or refuse to approach them about business in the first place? How do you build a business without alienating family and friends? Should you host home meetings or hotel meetings? *Can* you build your business online? Is it really possible to predict in advance whether or not a company will last?

A third set of questions has to do with the kinds of individuals involved in this particular field and the skills they need: What's the best strategy for recruiting boomers? Do you understand how and why so many women earn millions in this industry? How will you best overcome the inertia and fears that plague so many independent business owners? What absolutely vital habits drive networking success? What are the key competencies required to build a business? How can you deal with people and circumstances that stall your progress? How can you best lead, motivate, and serve your team? How do you overcome fears about rejection? Is it all about making money, or does networking go beyond the financial?

This book will address each of these questions, and provide you with proven, practical answers. It will also offer a series of tools to help you progress.

It's safe to say that, in all likelihood, we four authors will not be around in 2050, as our history greatly exceeds our future. And while it's impossible to look into a crystal ball and predict the future of capitalism, we can offer you an optimistic view of current reality and say with absolute certainty there has never been a better time to join our profession. How long that will be the case is anyone's guess; but it's possible today to create both wealth and time-freedom in network marketing.

This book is a paint-by-numbers strategy for you and your loved ones. All bets are off in a few years; but now more than ever before network marketing offers a legitimate wealth-creation opportunity. You hold in your hands a road map to dramatic success.

Stop believing the big lie, and realize that it *is* indeed possible to have both quality of life and quantity of stuff. You need not abandon one for the other. I've listened to all the excuses for 25 years. Some of my closest friends have ridiculed me for "doing one of those dumb pyramid deals." But many people have wasted their lives fighting traffic every day for the last 25 years while I've spent mine at home. Most people I've encountered over my lifetime have never even held a passport; I've gone through two and had to add pages to both because they became so filled with stamps from the immigration officials in countless nations on every continent.

It wasn't a degree that afforded me the opportunity to teach a college certification program in network marketing. It wasn't college classes in journalism that enabled me to write an international best seller. And it wasn't a lucky Wall Street stock speculation that resulted in enough wealth to live for an entire year in Gstaad, Switzerland. It wasn't political connections that granted my wife, Valerie, and me the opportunity to sit in Bill and Hilary Clinton's box seats in an opera house in Ukraine. And it wasn't wealthy parents who funded our family yacht trip through the British Virgin Islands with good friends.

We could write an entire chapter on the hidden assets of a career in network marketing—not the least of which is the lifelong friendships we develop in the process. For us, there's no greater example than the Tennessee family of Donnie and Dianne Walker, their kids and grandkids. We were briefly in a company together years ago and then went in different directions. Yet we stay in touch regularly, share the same values, and make it a point to spend quality time together. We couldn't put a price tag on how much we value their friendship. In our world, friendships are far more valuable adult "report cards" than money. The Walkers are great network marketers and wonderful human beings. Thanks to network marketing, they have touched our personal world.

All those wonderful experiences have come to us compliments of network marketing. You hold in your hands a book based on the cumulative wisdom of decades spent in this wonderful profession. What you do with the information is entirely up to you, but permit me one humble observation: As great as my life has been, I could have done two times more in half the time had I been able to read about and study this material first, as opposed to learning it through trial and error. I didn't have this road map, but you do. Read it, apply it—and we'll see you on the beaches of the world.

Part I

WHY NETWORK MARKETING?

I n Part I, we will prepare you for those philosophical questions and answers so necessary for success in our profession. Many people have false stereotypical images about network marketing, which must be addressed and those who pick up this book in order to evaluate our industry should be prepared to change their thinking. In fact, many professional networkers will benefit from a review of the fundamental mind-sets so critical to long-term success. Some veterans will have never seen these philosophical concepts explained in this manner.

The truths are these: Nobody has to alienate her friends and family, and boomers have no need to fear retirement. Nobody has to ever again be hampered by financial limitations nor should anyone ever again have challenges picking a viable company. Ours is a profession of equal opportunity for everyone and in spite of global economic problems that affect many folks, ours is a field that can thrive in bad times as well as good.

The reason many great people get into financial trouble in every sector of capitalism including ours is the fact that tacit wisdom is not transferrable. Tacit wisdom is that knowledge gained through hands-on experience in a specific domain. No matter how much we know about real estate, education, or insurance, there is absolutely no way that we can expect our philosophical considerations derived from those professions to benefit us in a field as different as network marketing. Part I of this book will alter your thinking and that is the critical factor so often ignored by most other books.

1

HOW A GROWING INDUSTRY CAN MAKE YOU RICH

Mark Yarnell

Radical wealth through network marketing starts with a critical decision that must reflect the core values and personality style of each participant. Simply put, some people are very comfortable with high-risk endeavors, while others prefer to undertake more stable circumstances. Pick the wrong company and you are hooped from day one. And it's not about money; it has much more to do with finding balance and harmony in one's core values and work ethics.

For example, John Terhune is a consummate professional in multiple business and legal sectors. I met him through a mutual friend who felt we had much in common. Although we are in different organizations, we have enjoyed his friendship and learned a great deal from him. If anyone has the personality, credibility, and competencies to thrive in international network marketing, it's this legal scholar/prosecuting attorney from the American South. During his third year of law school, John won the award as the Best Student Trial Advocate in the nation in a competition sponsored by the American Trial Lawyers Association. In his eight years as a Florida prosecutor, he won 98 percent of all his cases and served as chief of the entire Felony Division. I think it's safe to say that a man of his stature has the capacity to perform effective due diligence.

In fact, if anyone were capable of succeeding in any network marketing company—whether new or well established—it would be John Terhune. John enrolled in a 30-year-old stable company when he launched his networking career, and immediately began to rise through the qualification ranks, until, in record time, he achieved an extremely impressive promotional or leadership level. But unlike many others who did everything conceivable to hit a rank only one time, John achieved it consistently each year for half a decade—an accomplishment that qualified him to fly all over the world as a speaker/expert.

John explained to us that while the recognition and travel were marvelous, they never quite translated into the kind of income or personal fulfillment he had been seeking. He told us he felt like a young trailblazer trapped in a world of elderly settlers. While his colleagues, who were at or below his level of achievement, were out earning him by millions, John was making little more from the company he was representing than the amount he was spending on travel. After five years, he had basically made it to the break-even point in terms of income, while others at his level were building fortunes. It just didn't make sense.

One day while attending a corporate function, John decided to ask several of the organization's veterans why—and how—they were making so much more money than he was, in spite of the fact that they were all at similar pin levels (i.e., leadership levels). Without hesitation, one of the "good ole boys" offered him a one-word explanation that put it all in perspective; he looked at John and said, *"Timing."* That single word was the game-changer for John. He came to realize that he was indeed a pioneer stuck in a world of settlers. Those who had blazed the trail in his company three decades earlier were always going to be light years ahead of him financially, and they admitted it.

Imagine how the explorers Lewis and Clark would have felt under similar circumstances. What if they had crested a foothill in what is today Colorado and come face-to-face with a valley full of

50,000 men, women, and children? Now imagine that after arriving, the pair sought out the group's leaders, only to discover that they'd been in the valley for years, and that a number of others in their party had already reached the West Coast. Do you think after discovering this fact that these great adventurers would have continued westward and *pretended* to be trailblazers? Of course not.

Neither did John. As soon as he realized that the trail had already been blazed in his former company, he left to seek out greater challenges.

Today, John is a pioneer in a young venture. He's already earning a small fortune for his efforts; more important, he is enjoying the risk, adventure, and uncertainty that trailblazers find to be so fulfilling and vital. The financial rewards will be staggering when his company matures.

But, as I said in the Introduction, money isn't the only adult "report card." Instead, one of John's greatest rewards has been the opportunity to train other pioneers. Most of us derive serenity and personal satisfaction more from our journey than from our arrival at some preconceived, arbitrary destination. That's why it's so very important to pick a company that matches one's personality type. In fact, those who pick incompatible companies will generally fail, and certainly never thrive or achieve fulfillment. Even if they receive pin-level recognition early, the process itself will often prove unfulfilling. John is a prime example of this: Though he picked a stable company for his first vehicle, it just didn't offer him the chance to express his pioneering spirit. So he summoned the courage to blaze a different trail.

As we've learned more about human psychology, a very interesting character trait has become apparent in individuals who tend toward network marketing. The trailblazer thrives on adventure and risk; he or she cannot possibly feel exhilarated working in a long-term, stable company. In contrast, the settler generally feels very uncomfortable in a ground-floor, higher-risk venture. Regardless, some settlers want to *feel* like gutsy trailblazers, and some trailblazers want to *feel* like settlers or stable professionals. Unfortunately, it's seldom a good idea to make a career choice based on wishful thinking.

It's common for a settler to be seduced into joining an upstart venture by a competent recruiter because, as we've pointed out, most risk-averse people would *like* to be more adventurous. Likewise, many a trailblazer has been persuaded into a long-term stable company by an articulate family member or friend. Candidates see the huge checks earned by people who've been involved with a company since the early days, and come to believe that they can achieve the same payoff without having to face the upstart risks that early adopters encountered. They are told that although they missed the first big wave of momentum, they can still enjoy the wealth produced by catching the second wave.

We make no judgments about companies, whether they are upstart launches or long-term corporations. They can both be fabulous. In fact, *every* stable company was once a risky upstart. But we want you to understand from the very beginning that your company choice should reflect who you *are*—not who you hope to become. Why chase after the potential huge checks of an upstart venture— especially since we all know that most companies fail—if you are averse to risk and loss? On the other hand, why would you join a stable company with leaders on every continent, and settle for substantially less reward than those who joined 10 years earlier, if you are *not* threatened by failure and would love the gamble and adventure involved in taking a shot at the big money?

How do trailblazers get seduced into a company of settlers? It's simple. They tune out the needs of prospects and focus solely on their own. Some snakes in suits gravitate toward stable companies, while others join upstarts. A well-known example from recent headlines should put this fact of human nature in perspective for you. When notorious stockbroker Bernie Madoff's Ponzie scheme was exposed, a huge number of wealthy, successful professionals emerged as victims, many of whom lost millions. A large percentage of them were celebrities, both wealthy and well connected. Almost every one of them interviewed expressed the same dismay; over and over, they asserted, "Madoff was so believable. The returns were so far beyond other investment strategies that I was willing to gamble my assets." Some lost their entire retirement capital to this

seemingly kind, little old guy they called Uncle Bernie. Those people were risk takers. Many bet the farm in spite of the fact that the
expected returns were highly unrealistic.

The same problems exist in network marketing. Remember,
anyone can join any company at any time, and there's a miniscule
cash outlay for involvement. Very few companies expect people to
invest more than a few hundred dollars for products. In spite of the
huge upside potential and relatively minor risk, people use numerous and humorous excuses to avoid our profession. Some settlers
pretend that they have to talk to their spouses to get permission to
invest a tiny amount of money, while others insist on "trying" the
products—even when there's overwhelming scientific evidence to
prove that they work.

Conversely, whether investments or direct selling opportunities,
trailblazers think nothing of throwing investment capital into dubi-
ous gambles so long as their return is potentially huge. It essentially
comes down to varying personality styles. Statistically speaking, network marketing companies do not fail at a higher rate than companies in other industries. But believing they do is a common fallback
position for people who are looking for an excuse not to participate
in them. We saw a relevant bumper sticker on a Cadillac convert-
ible in Vancouver that reads, "Work is for people afraid to do network marketing." Many networkers detest structured work; some of
us fear it.

Equally critical is people's ability to dissect an opportunity intel-
ligently and perform proper due diligence once they've selected
the company category (established or upstart) that best fits their
psychological profile. So evaluate your personality style in regard
to risk, and ask the right questions about companies so that you can
determine whether or not they might be a good fit for you.

Until now, few trainers or authors have addressed the subject of
conducting company due diligence for fear of alienating independent business owners/distributors who have made poor company
choices. Why rock the boat if the goal is to sell books? Well, here's
why: Far too many people join companies, fail, and spend the rest of
their adult lives denigrating a potentially lucrative profession—when

they're the ones to blame for failing to ask the right questions in the first place. We are weary of hearing people denigrate a great profession and distribution model because of their own poor choices. For every trailblazer like John Terhune who figures this stuff out and starts over in a company that better matches his talents, dozens simply quit and bad-mouth the entire industry. And it's truly amazing how many spirited trailblazers hang around a dead company because the cadaver is still twitching.

Every field has its Bernie Madoffs and Warren Buffets, both financial planners and investment experts. Until regulators started asking the right questions, both Bernie and Warren were considered respectable members of the same profession. Let's just say that one of them is now eating a lot more macaroni and Spam than the other. We will teach you how to ask the right questions so that you can navigate safely away from pyramid schemes and toward legitimate upstarts. The regulators have guidelines that you need to know. What's even more important—given there are good and bad companies in both categories—is your ability to match your talents and competencies to the right vehicle.

We live in a world of constant change brought about by the Internet and other dynamics. The paradigm shift in how we communicate will forever affect the way we spend our well-earned money and how we choose to allocate our time. The Internet has become a virtual treasure trove for consumers who prefer to buy products conveniently and in the privacy of their own homes. No longer do we need to fight traffic and crowds to visit the local store; and buying on the Internet is almost an automatic process when one has to search for an unusual item.

This change in our buying habits is also fueling the growth of the network marketing model throughout the world. Many experts predict that our distribution model will enjoy unprecedented growth and acceptance within the next 5 to 10 years. Marketers will increasingly appreciate the value of face-to-face selling, compared to the huge costs for retail slotting fees and the millions of dollars spent on product rollouts and advertising.

After we teach you how to evaluate companies, we will get down to business. You deserve to know exactly how ordinary people achieve extraordinary residual income.

We are four adventurers who have earned substantial checks, governed multibillion-dollar international corporations, worked at the top levels of strategic business planning, mentored and coached many high-level entrepreneurs, and chaired numerous charitable organizations. We're prepared to teach you how to become a thriving entrepreneur and how to build a highly successful business—in spite of all the landmines and cow pies you'll encounter along the way.

We all chose the world of high-stakes network marketing as our last rodeo. It's not just what we write about; it's what we study and practice 24/7. We are hands-on participants in this wonderful profession, and we have succeeded dramatically by applying what you are about to learn.

This book comes to you at precisely the right time. Learn the principles we detail in it and you will be able to capitalize on the convergence of multiple megatrends that will drive your business success. What began in 2011 and will continue for 19 years is startling. Each day, 10,000 baby boomers turn 65, and less than 15 percent of this aging population is financially prepared for retirement. Simply put, many of these people worked hard, sacrificed much, and bet on a system that was built on bubbles instead of steel. Most will face a final few years of economic chaos unless they can find a viable way of making up for lost income in a timely way.

An even larger number of ambitious young people are emerging from the fog of hyperextended adolescence and are looking for a healthy work/life balance in a meaningful career. Millions of people need money—and they need it immediately.

We have the solution, and it requires very little capital, absolutely no experience, and no college degree. Network marketing offers radical wealth to those who can select a good company at the right time, put on blinders for a couple of years, and focus their energy and time in one direction without meaningless distractions. We need to marginalize—perhaps even eliminate—the multitasking myths that plague many. If you know what you're doing, entering the right network marketing company anytime between 2011 and 2031 will prove to be a profitable decision of unprecedented magnitude.

The choices you make over the next couple of decades will dramatically affect those you love for generations to come. Those of us who fully understand network marketing are amazed at how the stars have lined up so uniformly for our profession and this model for effectively taking products to market.

There has never been—and may never be again—a more ideal international climate for success as an entrepreneur. Certainly, there have never been fewer reliable options for rapid capital accumulation. Real estate, Wall Street, hedge funds, and other financial vehicles have declined in popularity because so many sociopaths at the top have morphed into full-blown snakes in suits.

If what we describe in this book you are now holding makes sense, take action. We'll teach you precisely what to do; the rest is up to you. And remember, it all begins with the selection process. You must align yourself with an organization that matches who you *are—not* who you want to be. Trailblazers who join mature, stable companies, and settlers who join upstart, risky ventures, set themselves up for disappointment and failure.

Chapter 2

NETWORK MARKETING FOR BOOMERS

Retirement Plan B

Mark Yarnell

Obviously, none of us is blessed with the ability to gaze into a crystal ball and predict the future. But it is very easy to state with certainty that those of us born between 1946 and 1964—we 70 million-plus "boomers"—are facing some economically volatile final years. Members of our generation are trying desperately to whip the retirement dragon, a two-headed monster that's forcing us to confront two daunting issues: boredom and financial uncertainty.

We were all exposed to the same song and dance as children, a song repeated so often that we all committed it to memory. In fact, if we merely wrote the first two words, you would immediately remember the rest of the lyrics and the melody as well. As we aged, many of us began, unwittingly, to view our final years through the filter of that simple childhood rhyme. We believed that if we rowed our boats "gently down the stream," the payoff would be a life in which a few golden years would be filled with marvelous rewards like grandchildren, golf, and fly-fishing. We promised ourselves a final chapter of serenity and fulfillment—a vision that, for many, has become little more than a pipe dream. Here's why.

After paddling our metaphorical kayaks through 40 years of turbulent white water, we came ashore near that beautiful old-growth forest called retirement only to come face-to-face with a two-headed, fire-breathing dragon called Theidleboresus Rex. That name alone speaks volumes. As previously stated, this monster is composed of twin volatilities: unproductive idle time and unanticipated capital depletion. What no one taught us as we were navigating through those career years was that the greatest challenges awaited us near the *end* of the journey. As we rounded the final bend in the stream and drifted into calm waters, Theidleboresus Rex awakened from his lair. He prepared to engage us in that final epic battle: retirement. No one has slain this dragon throughout the history of humanity, although a few of us have gotten the better of him.

You can't pull out a two-iron or fly rod and slay the dragon. But you can get the better of Theidleboresus Rex with the proper strategic plan. The four of us are among the few who have managed to outwit the dragon, and we'll teach you exactly how we did it. Keep in mind it's not about fight or flight at our age. We've accumulated enough wisdom by retirement to soar like eagles—that is, if we use our heads. Flight is the only sane option, and network marketing is the best vehicle.

We discovered an erroneous mind-set that leads many boomers directly into the dragon's lair: Productive people can derive fulfillment from unproductive activities. Simply put, most can't. Over the years we have seen countless individuals attempt to slay the dragon with everything from golf clubs to fishing rods. Unfortunately, tools of leisure seldom fulfill one's inherent need to be productive.

Consider the great game of golf. So long as golf was an occasional payback for numerous hours of productivity, it remained extremely fulfilling. The same was true of fishing, tennis, paragliding, and a multitude of other hobbies and amusements. Unfortunately, they all soon lose their novelty when we engage in them with regularity.

There is no real measurable payoff in amateur behavior—which is a big problem for anyone accustomed to receiving the two adult report cards of money and respect. No matter how big the sweet spot, a Big Bertha driver cannot deliver either to most of us. The same applies to an $800 Winston three-piece fly rod, a $5,000 paraglider, or a powerful ski boat. Tools created for amusement cannot be used to slay the retirement dragon. Many folks put up a good fight in the short term; but none win, and all die trying.

Some folks attempt the geographic cure. They're like the drunk who decides to move to another city and make new friends in order to quit drinking. Many formerly productive retirees believe that joining a more expensive country club or flying to remote areas of Alaska to fish will somehow make a difference. All that kind of behavior does is provide temporary solutions to permanent problems. Changing locations will not end alcoholism any more than moving to a new country or buying a bigger boat will defeat boredom. We boomers need to be challenged. Much like overcoming alcoholism, getting the best of boredom requires a change in behavior, not geography. Golf and fishing are the same activities in remote locations as they are a few miles from home, just as there are as many bars and drunks in every community as there are in one's hometown.

The first requirement for anyone who is serious about besting the retirement dragon is to make a simple cognitive adjustment. After four decades of white-water rafting through dangerous and exciting career rapids, it makes perfect sense to pull ashore for a breather. A bit of golf or trout fishing is certainly reasonable—and deserved. But before the two-headed retirement dragon awakens and begins breathing the twin fires of boredom and financial problems in your direction, you need to reevaluate your basic assumptions about the alleged "golden years." Unless you are ready to surrender and face defeat, you'll need to continue to prioritize some form of effort above leisure. Network marketing offers the perfect challenge.

Most of us by retirement age have the wisdom and capacity to be remarkably productive by working smarter rather than harder. We have the brains; all we need is the vehicle. I've heard it expressed another way: "Most people over age 55 are Ferraris looking for cans of gas." Boomers want to be challenged *and* productive. We have three options: We can attempt to slay the dragon by courageously engaging in battle. We can surrender and die. Or we can climb into a new kayak and reenter the white water.

The four of us chose the third option, and we are going to attempt to persuade you to do the same. Why? For starters, no one—especially at our age—can slay a four-ton, fire-breathing dragon. So option one is irrational, and option two is absurd. Who wants to surrender and die early? Simply put, those who select either of these will soon be gone. Option three extends life measurably and maximizes one's fulfillment. The only way to get the better of that dragon is to grab a new vessel and push back into the white water. And we would prefer to avoid boredom while doing so. Keep this in mind, regardless of whether you are a boomer or a younger person trying to interest a prospect who is a member of the baby boom sector.

The second problem is the dragon's head we fear most: financial uncertainty. Playing by the rules didn't work for most boomers because of numerous circumstances outside our influence. A lot of things changed dramatically in the last few years—and not just in North America. Global economics are changing, and at warp speed. The "safe investments" that we thought would provide decent retirement lifestyles have shrunk dramatically. Many of my friends who minimized risks have lost everything—and in most cases it wasn't because of irrational investments. One of my relatives put over half of his retirement capital in Enron right after that company appeared on the cover of *Forbes* magazine for a sixth year and was touted as one of "America's most trusted companies." There was nothing risky or irrational about that stock play. But he lost, and lost big time. And one of my very conservative friends spent years accumulating positive cash flow properties. When many of his friends started to make a killing by flipping rental houses, Arthur jumped into the game. In spite of years of experience, he lost every penny of equity in 24 months and now faces a grim final few years, which he planned on spending in relative comfort.

Wall Street snakes and small-time, unethical stockbrokers lured many baby boomers unwittingly into high-stakes investment strategies fueled by greed and irrational speculation. One formerly conservative friend lost his home after telling me that he was making a killing in online day trading. I never found out the whole truth because after his wife left him, he moved to Puerto Rico and none of us has heard from him in over a year. I know he's a bit embarrassed—and I can only hope he is still alive and well.

Although we can't predict the long-term future, we can make one short-term assumption with considerable certainty: Unless they take immediate action, boomers are hosed. The final group of boomers to turn 65 will do so in 2029. On average, they will live another 20 years, which puts the end of the boomer retirement threshold at 2049.

There is a window of opportunity for professional network marketing between today and 2049, and it is open wider than any other in history. Why? Because virtually everybody in the aging boomer generation needs retirement capital in a hurry—and all their options have been eliminated by a small minority of sociopathic snakes in suits. It has become nearly impossible to overestimate the greed of many in the financial sector.

There are also the local, state, and federal politicians who accept legal bribes from lobbyists, as well as the lawyers who use jurisprudence to acquire huge retainers and lopsided fees from the most vulnerable among us—leaving the majority of clueless middle-class citizens with little more than the token joy they can get from Facebook, Twitter, and video games. Like zombies from *Night of the Living Dead*, wireless addicts line the streets, malls, and airports staring at little WiFi feed drips of irrelevant minutiae. Morons who try to multitask at 60 mph kill thousands of innocent drivers and pedestrians weekly.

The point of all this is fairly simple: Network marketing is the only game in town for the next four decades, because it's the fastest way to accumulate risk-free wealth in large enough increments to enable boomers to retire comfortably. This cannot be done in real estate without significant capital; nor can it be done in mutual funds, gold, or silver. And it cannot be done, except by a handful of mathematical wizards, online or offline by trading in any markets or currency.

Boomers are doomed—unless they become willing to explore new opportunities. And here's the good news: Boomers are finally willing to do exactly that.

We have discovered a marvelous fact over the past few years. In today's economy, baby boomers are willing to overlook their stereotypical assumptions about network marketing when it is presented professionally and ethically to them. Many will actually pull the trigger and engage in our business if their due diligence verifies what you tell them.

Most boomers are savvy. They have lived a lot of years and learned a lot of lessons. Many are well equipped with BS detectors as a direct result of their numerous encounters with snake oil sales experts. A good number of boomers have dabbled in more than one network marketing venture and failed. They can smell a rotten deal a mile away, because they or someone they love has ended up with a garage full of crap. Worse, some who drank the Kool-Aid used their credibility to bring friends and family members into foolish deals only to have those poor souls wind up with garages full of crap themselves. Many people are jaded, for good reasons. But many also are willing to listen to you if what you are proposing makes sense.

We want to arm you with a legitimate strategy—one that, fortunately, is not very complicated. The first step is to make certain that the products you will be touting to boomers have been scientifically validated. You should also make an effort to consume them yourself.

Next, make certain that your initial approach creates enough of a conscious shock to compel your prospect to pay attention.

Finally, make certain that you convey the *truth* about your company's ground-floor opportunity or long-term stability. Never exaggerate the safety of an upstart venture or the income potential of a mature company. Stress the assets of your company's timing, rather than fabricating rewards that are unattainable or risky.

The reason so many boomers have been resistant to our industry is because they have been lied to about the risk, the income potential, or both. People my age can smell a rat a mile away, so don't waste your time trying to make an otherwise sensible opportunity into something it isn't.

Let's examine the specific steps in boomer prospecting and recruiting, as this demographic comprises the largest market sector of people who must take immediate action. And if you want to chase younger people, by all means, have at it. Grab a BlackBerry, skateboard, and nose ring, and poof! Everyone under 40 is a target. But remember, it's boomers who are just a few years away from the Tranquility Hills Manor, where many will be playing bingo for a toaster oven, with oatmeal dribbling down their chins, instead of putting on the eighteenth green for a bottle of $80 single-malt whiskey. And they know it.

There are two specific areas of interest to cover when approaching a boomer: big money and free time. I'm not talking about chump-change, like $3,000 a month. I'm talking about three to five units of principle-less interest—which is monthly income tied directly to consumer products rather than financial instruments.

Most boomers don't have a big whack of liquid capital; even if they did, the only safe place for it is under their mattresses. And chances are that they don't want to risk what little they have left. One unit is $10,000; so three to five units is $30,000 to $50,000 a month. Who doesn't want to cash flow *that*? The trick, however, is to explain it from the outset in units of principle-less interest. A good question is this: "Uncle Bob, how would you like to create three to five units of principle-less interest in under two years without any risk?" I'll guarantee you that Uncle Bob will ask you some questions—because he has no idea what you just asked *him*.

Now if you ask Uncle Bob if he would like to see the ultimate ground-floor home business, he'll tell you to take a hike. Why? Because even though some boomers are uninformed they think they know all about network marketing. And to them, the terms "home business" or "residual income" are synonymous with network marketing.

So don't invite a stereotypical reaction with red-flag terminology. It's not that you want to be deceptive or misleading; but if you use phrases that immediately give boomers reason to pause, you will fail because of your approach. However, if you use synonyms that mean the same thing, you might be able to help your prospect avoid a pathetic retirement.

Once your prospect becomes curious, it's time to guide him or her to an introductory website or prerecorded message that's specifically designed to tweak his or her interest without going into any great detail. Use a short, generic exposure tool offered by your own company or like the one I posted at www.15yearsleft.com. If you give prospects a corporate website on first contact and turn them loose to do their own self-presentation, you will generally lose them. Better to direct them to a brief overview of global economics or network marketing and ask them to call you back if they are interested in learning more. Remember these terms: *units of principle-less interest* tied to a *proprietary funding vehicle*. By that, we mean *patented technology*.

If your company has patented products, customers will have to reorder through your distributors. Being able to buy a similar product at any health food store or Costco does not engender the customer loyalty or reorders that are essential to passive residual income.

Most boomers understand the absurdities inherent in derivatives and other investment tricks played by the financial sector. Your goal is to explain how much more *sane* it is to tie retirement income to consumable products, rather than to risky speculative schemes. It's up to you to teach them about that option.

Even programmer Richard Brodie, creator of Microsoft Word, calls network marketing the "business model of the future" in his latest best seller *Virus of the Mind*. If you can present network marketing properly to a few boomers every day, you will be earning sizable checks in less than two years. Of course, that's assuming you have joined a company with proprietary products, competent management, and a seamless global comp plan.

Every age group is crammed with people who are disillusioned and debt-ridden. But boomers facing the retirement dragon no longer enjoy the luxury of having several productive decades ahead of them. Members of our generation need to take action—and we need to do so before we fall victim to financial depletion and boredom. Boomers must act fast, and most know it.

The most troubling fact of all is that most retirement-age people have run out of options. Network marketing is the last bastion of free enterprise for those of us who have come face-to-face with the retirement dragon. So by all means, talk to people of every age group about your opportunity, but keep in mind that it's boomers who need our industry more than any other demographic. I can promise you that none of us wants to die playing Grand Theft Auto or bingo.

Chapter 3

THE MOST IMPORTANT DECISION IN NETWORK MARKETING

Choosing the Right Company

Derek Hall

I can't think of a time in my career when I needed to muster every single one of my skills more than when I was deciding whether to accept a job offer. Yet, if you're like me, you too have accepted a position based on the financial package and job title alone. I have done this without bothering to conduct much due diligence on the company—including its financial stability. How crazy is *that*? After all, what good is a great job or a fancy title if the company is not sustainable for any length of time? Those of you who have experienced what I went through know that it's not something you'd like to repeat. If there is any consolation at all, it would be that you learned a lesson you'll never forget.

Choosing a network marketing company is not unlike choosing a new job. Therefore, the goal of this chapter is to cover some reasonably easy checks and balances as part of a due diligence process you should complete *before* you throw your heart and soul into a new business venture.

WHO'S RUNNING THE SHOW?

The first step in this process is to check out the owners and others who are running the business. In today's world of accessible information it's fairly easy to type one or more names into a search engine and see what pops up. And because nothing ever *completely* goes away once it has appeared on the Internet, it's not unusual that information your search turns up may be quite old and irrelevant to your current needs; nevertheless, you generally will unearth a valuable nugget from among all the throwaway material that can help you with your decision.

You're not necessarily looking for unfavorable reports on the owners—though that would certainly be informative; you should be more interested in the companies they have participated in previously, and whether they were successful at them. You also want to uncover what positions the owners held at these other companies, as this might indicate whether they are truly qualified leaders, capable of running the current business successfully.

You should be looking for indications of current or past legal problems as well, to make sure no potential costly settlement is in the offing that could affect the company's financial stability. Sometimes I wish the United States embraced some of the nuances of the British legal system; in the United Kingdom, if you are sued by someone and you prevail in the case, the plaintiff is responsible not just for any damages to the defendant, but also for the defendant's legal costs, as well as his or her own. As we all know, the U.S. legal system allows us to sue another person or entity for *anything*, and we are responsible for our own defense costs whether we win or lose the case. The only way we can recover those costs is to spend more money on legal fees to conduct a countersuit. I mention this because lawsuits are endemic to the business of doing business in the United States. We cannot and should not assume that a lawsuit against a person equates to his or her inability to run a business.

Use the available information you gather wisely; resist the temptation to jump to conclusions. Learn as you can, to enable you to make a well-balanced decision. Ask yourself, "Does the negative material I have found detract from the company's ability to grow and prosper for the next 50 years?" And, "Does my face-to-face meeting with the owners or top distributors trump the information I dug up on the Internet?"

Also be sure to check references for the individuals at companies you are investigating. Even though it's rare for a reference to give a negative referral for a former employee, by asking the right questions you can glean what you need to know in just a few minutes. Questions regarding term of employment, nature of the role and position held are completely appropriate. New companies crop up every day, and as long as the people who work for them can develop a solution to a problem or provide a service that meets a need or fills a void, they will thrive. Unfortunately, not all companies meet a sustainable need; some fade away or simply close their doors after just a year or two. Network marketing companies rely heavily on their top field leadership to blaze the trail in the early days. They then provide motivational direction to the field organization as it gains momentum, and later on as the company enters its maintenance stage.

These field leaders (often referred to as *master distributors*) can either make or break a company, so it's crucial that you carefully examine the backgrounds of at least a few of them before you decide to join the organization. If the company you are investigating is relatively new, it's of critical importance that you look long and hard at the field leaders. Some companies may have only one master distributor, while others might have a few more. Do your research and learn as much as you can about them. Look into these leaders' experience. For instance, if a particular master distributor has moved from one company to another multiple times over the past few years, you probably want to question whether this is someone upon whom you can rely for any sustainable period of time.

Another concern are the network marketing companies that have a history of offering large sums of money to high-powered distributors who have enjoyed success at other firms. Such a company essentially hopes that once on board a "big gun" will then convince a large number from his or her previous organization to also join the new firm. However, even a cursory glance at the industry's track record will prove to you these higher-ups are rarely able to successfully transfer their former organizations to their new ones. The more likely scenario is that they gladly accept the up-front money from the new company, but generally fail to reproduce their previous success; in fact, they often leave after a short time in search of an even more lucrative opportunity. When you see this pattern in a company—either at the corporate level or in the field—turn and run, as fast as you can, because it spells trouble every time.

During my tenure as a business manager, I have studiously avoided hiring anyone with a record of short stays at various companies because I know there is usually a reason for such a pattern; therefore, I never make this mistake. I recommend you use the same logic as you conduct your due diligence to find a network marketing company; and by all means, spend the necessary time to determine who holds the key positions.

START-UP OR STABLE?

There is a significant difference between a company that has been around for decades and a start-up. There's no question that a newer firm is loaded with risks. That said, and as history has borne out, many start-ups have been the genesis of extreme wealth for millions of people who "got in early." For example, wouldn't you have liked to own Microsoft stock in the early days of its development? Or to have worked for Sam Walton in the early sixties when he was handing out shares of the company rather than salaries to his key employees? Those early employees shared Walton's future vision of what eventually became Walmart—not only the world's largest retailer today, but the largest business overall—and became extremely wealthy along the way. Each of these companies was a start-up at one time; good timing and the compelling vision of their founders carried them through difficult times to astronomical growth.

This part of your due diligence will be the most difficult if the company you're investigating is either privately held or a start-up. Nevertheless, you must do your homework as thoroughly as you can. You don't want to enter into what appears to be a promising relationship only to eventually be disappointed and discouraged.

The financial capital required to launch a network marketing company is often much less than the amount needed to start a conventional wholesale/retail model, so it can easily attract very talented but underfunded entrepreneurs. These opportunists often come armed with very enticing business plans (and, often, unrealistic expectations). All of them have the potential and intent to attract independent distributors who are looking for an opportunity to make easy money, and make it fast. Don't get trapped by such short-term opportunities. Again, do your homework; look for the telltale signs that can keep you from making a bad decision.

Here are a few guidelines to help you head off a possible disaster in the making.

First, arrange a meeting with one or more of the company's owners or founders, or even a senior officer. If you find even this initial step to be at all difficult—or if one or more of the company officials decline your visit—regard it as a very important clue that the company culture may be suspect.

Before you meet with the company official(s), jot down a dozen or so questions whose answers are crucial to your decision. The following is a list of questions I suggest you ask for a privately held company. If the company you are investigating is public then most information you seek will be easy to obtain. Though it's certainly not all-inclusive, it will give you a good start on your preparation.

1. How is the company capitalized—by the owners or by outside investors?
2. How much of the company is owned by the founders/owners?
3. What's the plan to fund future growth?
4. Does the company have access to additional capital to fund rapid growth?
5. Does the company have an adequate line of credit to support erratic growth?
6. Does the company have debt; if so, what is the ratio of that debt to assets?

7. Does the company have any outstanding legal concerns, such as unresolved lawsuits or product liability issues?
8. What is the previous experience of the chief financial officer and/or the chief executive officer?
9. Has the company ever filed for bankruptcy protection?
10. Is the company willing to let you review a copy of its most recent year-end financial report? If not, be sure to ask whether the annual statement is audited by a reputable accounting firm.
11. What is the company's long-term business plan?
12. What are the company's current annual net sales; and more important, at what rate are they increasing?
13. In what area of business is the company currently investing its capital?

Chances are you won't receive adequate answers to all of these questions; that's just the nature of a privately held company. However, if you don't ask, you won't learn anything. And if you pose your questions in a professional manner, as opposed to seeming to be on a "fishing expedition," you will definitely get answers to some of them. When pieced together, these responses will give you a fairly detailed portrait of the company, from which you can draw your conclusions.

GROWING OR MATURING?

Another important part of your due diligence process will be to analyze the organization's growth pattern. In other words, you must determine where the company is in its life cycle. It will be most important to learn whether it has gone through the rapid growth stage called *momentum* or is in the early stages of building a solid foundation from which it plans to accelerate growth. Maybe the company has completed the initial development phase and is maturing into a solid company, one that's maintained growth for several years. This information will help you decide which model suits your needs. Though greater wealth often comes to those who get in early, this period is fraught with more risk; only you know your appetite for risk. A premomentum company is, necessarily, a higher risk; at the same time, it presents the opportunity for higher returns over the long term. A more mature company that has already grown will still provide a steady income, but probably not offer the same level of wealth potential.

I cannot overemphasize the need to gather as much information as you can about the company's financial status as you continue your search. You can easily obtain data on public organizations from the public record; this is more difficult for privately held organizations.

If you are fortunate enough to receive a financial summary or financial trend analysis (even an unaudited one), pay close attention to the trend in sales. Don't be concerned if sales are up one month and then dip somewhat in the next; many businesses are cyclical by nature. Rather, look carefully at the 6- or 12-month trend, to determine whether the general movement is up or down.

If the business seems to be on an upswing, find out why; believe it or not, not all business increases are healthy or positive. For instance, one network marketing company I know has been around for many years with a not-so-exciting product offering. Nevertheless, sales increased every year, but not because of existing market expansion or unit sales—which is the hallmark of true growth. In this case, it was due to the organization opening a division in a new country every year. Eventually, however, it ran out of new places in which to open, and the business began to slip backward. The lesson here is, don't look closely at just the sales numbers; ask about the details behind them, as well. Examine the profit line, and don't be misled by either a robust number or a weak number. It will be very difficult to determine all the components having an impact on the bottom line—and I can assure you that the company owners will not share all the minute details.

If company officials decline your request to review a financial summary, ask these questions:

- What is the sales trend?
- From where are new sales coming?

- Have new products been introduced recently; if so, to what extent are they impacting sales?
- Where is the concentration of the present sales growth?
- Is the company profitable now?
- Does the company have a positive cash flow?

Most new network marketing companies fail within the first year or two, for a variety of reasons, ranging from poor product to weak distributors and undercapitalization—to mention just a few. As stated previously, be aware of where the company is in its growth cycle *as you are examining it.*

Be sure, also, to analyze the countries where the company is officially doing business; this will have a substantial impact on your personal growth opportunity. Asia, specifically, is a veritable treasure trove for network marketing companies today; Japan, Taiwan, and Korea, and others are some of the best networking countries in the world. If the organization you are investigating has previously launched in these countries, it should weigh heavily in your decision-making process, as the major growth potential may have already passed.

IS THE PRODUCT PROVEN?

The days are long past when a business could launch and operate on hype alone; hundreds of such companies have come and gone. Today's consumers are much better educated and more wary than those of past generations. They are bombarded with information from all sides—and a lot of it stays with us and can help when we're making these critical decisions. It is thanks to this paradigm shift in our reasoning capabilities that companies are developing more meaningful products and services to fill a need and to attract new consumers. Network marketing companies are specifically developing marketing plans to attract both distributors and consumers.

I continue to be entertained by the number of TV commercials that feature a man or woman in a white coat explaining the benefits of a new product that can enhance your health. If you look closely at the bottom of the screen during these commercials, you will see the disclaimer (usually in very small type) that tells you the white-coated person is a paid actor, not an actual doctor or other expert in the field. If you hope to represent a product that purports to have a positive impact on the consumer, doesn't it make sense to involve real experts to explain and represent the benefits of the product?

Conduct sufficient research to make sure the product you are soon to begin distributing has been amply developed, formu-lated, and tested by the same experts who speak to the product's value. In the case of health products, for example, it is infinitely more important that the product be doctor-developed and not just doctor-endorsed. In your own situation, make sure the product will do what is claimed in the marketing plan. Any missing pieces of the product puzzle should send up a huge red flag. Consider the sup-porting science and research before you make your final decision — and don't be fooled by the slick marketing and hype. It is a sure prescription for failure.

Part of your investigation of a product offering should be to request, and then vet thoroughly, a few product testimonials; and, when possible, make contact with at least one or two of the people who've offered them. Hearing firsthand that the product does what it claims to do, and how it can change someone's lifestyle or daily routine for the better, will give you the peace of mind you need to make a wise decision. Every company tracks these kinds of endorse-ments, so never accept a firm's refusal to supply them.

WHAT'S THE SUPPORT SYSTEM?

I mentioned earlier the importance of doing in-depth research on the company owners. I restate here that this is a crucial a step in your a due diligence process. Equally important in the world of net-work marketing is the breadth of support you can get, and should expect, from the company's headquarters location. This site—and the group of people who work there—should serve as your total support system for a variety of functions. The beauty of today's networking business environment is that the majority of logistical functions are no longer your responsibility; they've become part of the headquarters support system.

This is very different from how network marketing companies used to be organized. Traditionally, distributors ordered goods from the company, stored them in a warehouse (or in their garage), and then disseminated the products to their customers. I have memories of friends working in the Amway and Avon businesses years ago; they always had a garage full of detergent or cosmetics. Thank goodness those days are gone, forever.

Today's company headquarters provide myriad services, from drop-shipping product direct to the distributor's customer to providing every type of training available, in both print and digital formats. They also offer billing and collection services, year-end accounting functions, personalized replicated websites, product sampling, collateral marketing materials, and much more. The distributor's role nowadays is to represent the company and its product, and leave the rest of the process to the company. When you consider the very low cost of entry for a distributor into a company, and to set up his or her own home-based business, it's no surprise that the networking model is growing so fast; and there can be no doubt that it will continue to outpace other business models for the foreseeable future.

WHAT'S THE COMPENSATION PLAN?

Be sure to investigate the array of services being offered before you make your decision to invest. Make sure the critical components are in place and functioning the way they should be. Specifically, the compensation plan is of critical importance. There are a variety of pay plans in the world of network marketing, and though all of them are built upon the basic idea of a multilevel system of earning commissions, not all plans are created equal. Therefore, you will need to determine which one will work best for you.

Many plans offer substantial front-loaded incentives in the form of cars, vacations, and fast cash, for one reason: to attract you. Be smart in conducting your review, and never lose sight of the fact that there is a finite amount of money available to pay out in these plans; the corporate entity must be able to cover its costs while also retaining a profit for its stakeholders, otherwise, it will cease to exist. Put more simply, there are many ways to slice the pie, but there is only one pie. Don't be fooled by enticing incentives; rather, look at the big picture and ask some of the company's veteran distributors whether the plan is living up to its promise for them.

Make sure as well that the compensation plan is compatible with the company's expansion into other countries. The term you'll hear used most often in discussions about international expansion is *seamlessness*. In other words, is the compensation plan flexible enough to accommodate international growth, and will it accommodate multiple foreign currencies; or will it be required to develop a different plan for each country? This is an important part of your research, and an easy question to ask along the way.

WHO MAKES AND SUPPLIES THE PRODUCT?

Many network marketing companies today align themselves with contract manufacturers that produce the product for them, while the company provides specifics and formulas. This is not a bad scenario; in fact, it is actually quite an effective approach, and here is why: Network marketing companies are almost always marketing companies first, and—in an ever-diminishing role—manufacturers of the goods they sell. Over the past 30 years or so, this new industry—referred to as the *contract manufacturing industry*—has grown into a multibillion-dollar segment of the process of taking a product to market.

These contractors often specialize in certain product formulas or unique manufacturing processes. They develop new ways to produce something less expensively, or formulate a new product that they hope to sell to their clients. This is all well and good; however, as in every other industry there are good players and there are bad ones. The good ones take the high ground and focus on quality; the low-ground companies cut corners and care more about price and profit than they do about quality.

The network marketing companies that are doing things right will spend years developing lasting relationships with their contracting partners. The partners, then, gain assurance over the years that their chosen companies take a quality-first approach; together, they put in place all the necessary checks and balances to assure that the end product is safe and effective. It's also important to mention here that most companies select more than one contractor with whom to do business. This serves the dual purpose of keeping the process competitive and guarding against inventory shortfalls or ingredient or component supply problems.

It would be virtually impossible for you to complete an in-depth study of all the suppliers used by the company you are considering joining; nevertheless, you *should* become familiar with the manufacturing process and strategy it employs. Once you have this information, use it to formulate appropriate questions to ask the company about the suppliers. It's also a good idea to request a tour of the contractor's manufacturing facility.

WHAT'S THE LONG-TERM OUTLOOK?

Finally, there are two additional important areas that you must investigate before making a decision to join a company: Determine (1) whether the company is sustainable and scalable, and (2) whether its marketing approach will continue to appeal to a broad customer base. Is the product offering limited to a single demographic? Is the pricing structure such that the consumer will continue to pay for the product or service 5, 10, or 20 years from now? Is the company locked into a narrow business core? Can the product offering be improved over the years, and expanded into a variety of offerings?

Consider as an example one very successful trend in network marketing of the past 15 years to launch companies based on what are commonly referred to as "super juices" or "super fruits." These so-called breakthrough juices are typically extracted from mysterious and exotic fruits such as the noni fruit from Polynesia and Southeast Asia or the acai berry from Central and South America. The companies selling these juices claim they have been the source of longevity and age-reversal for indigenous peoples for centuries. Unfortunately, there is minimal science and/or safety trials to back up most of these claims; instead, their marketers rely heavily upon empirical data, folklore, and impressive packaging. Several of these companies over the past two decades succeeded in attracting millions of distributors looking to cash in on the super juice phenomenon, and consequently, saw their sales soar at a tremendous rate. However, these products were rarely proprietary and before long every big-box store in the world began to carry their own versions of the super juices at a fraction of the prices charged by early-entry companies. This, ultimately, caused erosion of the sales bases of the various super juice network marketers—which continues today.

As retail competitors began to emerge, and the magic started to wear off for the networkers, marketers for these companies faced the difficult task of reinventing their firms to shore up falling sales. The problem was that they were "just juice" companies; in many cases, they had even named their corporations after the fruit, or a close facsimile of it. Thus, no matter what innovations they attempted to institute, they were still juice companies; for that reason, their sales continue to plummet today.

The lesson here? Be wary of companies that invest all their resources, reputation, capital—in effect, their entire future—in one product that it considers to be a "magic bullet." These businesses are rarely sustainable over a long period of time.

That said, many corporations have successfully reinvented themselves over the years and proved they are sustainable in any economic climate and can adjust to demographic shifts. A shining example is Target Corporation, which, after a few years of lagging growth, changed its image to appeal to a new type of consumer. Its successful evolution included commercials that featured trustworthy celebrity endorsers, and a marketing plan that became instantly recognizable to Target consumers by its bull's-eye logo—reminiscent of the Nike "swoosh."

Another company that has made a similar transformation to its product image is Cadillac, from an automaker that made cars that appealed to our parents and grandparents into one that now sells very sporty and highly trendy automobiles that attract a younger generation of buyers. Cadillac's new futuristic-looking cars have incredible drawing power and sex appeal, and cross all demographic lines.

It's also critical to consider *scalability* in your due diligence process. When it comes to network marketing, you need to know whether the business model will function across international boundaries. Will the product or service appeal not only to a North American consumer but to an Asian, South American, and European consumer as well? You also need to determine whether the offering is compatible with the various laws of other countries. And does the pricing structure enable citizens of less affluent countries to afford it? Is the product or service so unique that the growth it can attain in 5 or 10 years may be limited? It's important to gather enough facts in this regard so that you can draw some meaningful conclusions; otherwise, you may find yourself in a company with a limited future. Look hard at the product pipeline to determine how scalable the product strategy may be in the years to come.

In conclusion, do your homework. Don't rely solely on what you hear during a pitch at the company headquarters. Ask someone at the middle management level about the corporate culture. His or her answer will speak volumes about the company, and may also tell you where to look for other information you seek. Spend time, as well, with a field leader or two, and ask how they are treated; and while you're at it, confirm with them the facts you received at the corporate level. You will not regret taking these simple steps before choosing your future business partner.

Chapter 4

YOU DON'T HAVE TO ALIENATE FRIENDS AND FAMILY

Relationship Marketing and Family Matters

Shelby Hall

"Oh no, he's wearing those clothes again."

This was the remark our second son often made some years ago whenever he saw his father descending the stairs dressed in a certain pair of work boots, jeans, and a tee shirt. He and the rest of our children knew what to expect when their dad wore that particular outfit: It was Saturday, which meant yard work or a project. However, they also knew that after giving up two or three hours of their day to help, they would be rewarded at the end of it, usually with a barbeque and a swim party in the family pool.

If you think your personal routines and relationship development patterns are not contagious, think again. Our children now have grown children of their own and they are doing the very same things we did decades ago.

Ask yourself this question: How do people feel when they see you coming or hear your voice? Do they think, "Look out, here comes Jane, and I heard by way of the grapevine that she is building a business in one of those pyramid companies." What these individuals generally fail to realize is that they too work for companies whose employee organization charts look like a pyramid; and many likely attend churches whose hierarchy is pyramid shaped as well. The word "pyramid" coupled with the word "scheme" comprise a term used to describe an illegal venture wherein only those at the top of the pyramid make money and those at the bottom make none. Such schemes are synonymous with what are known today as Ponzi schemes, named after Charles Ponzi, who created a fraudulent investment operation that pays returns to its investors from their own money or the money paid by subsequent investors.

The organizational structure at network marketing companies does indeed have the appearance of a pyramid shape, but it is by no means illegal or fraudulent. In this chapter I describe our personal experiences in building lasting relationships with customers, friends, and neighbors, with a focus on what has worked for us through the years. I ask that you consider these ideas and test them in your own relationships, while keeping in mind that the process of building a network is virtually analogous to that of building a family.

We all come into this world with different personalities and character traits. There's a great book called *The Color Code* by Dr. Taylor Hartman (also known as *The Hartman Personality Profile*) that explores human relationships and understanding by way of dividing personalities into four categories defined by color: red (the power wielders), blue (the do-gooders), white (the peacekeepers), and yellow (the fun lovers). As a student of Dr. Hartman's work and philosophy—as well as a dear friend—I've learned a lot from him throughout the years. I have come to believe that identifying the color group into which you fit—as well as homing in on the personality color of others—makes it much easier to get along with them. Specifically, it comes as a huge help when you are considering their roles in your business building process.

We all have needs, wants, strengths, and weaknesses; and we must discover what drives us to act—or more important, *react*—in certain ways. Growing more familiar with our personality traits, as well as the traits of those around us, enables our relationships to become more genuine, longer lasting, and much more complete. We can, for example, begin to anticipate how a person will react in a particular situation and can, therefore, alleviate—or even avoid—those scenarios that will lead to trouble. It's really just human nature to "dodge the cow pies in the pasture" as we make our way through our life's experiences.

Though we can choose our friends and our business partners, we cannot choose who takes up residence on the various branches on our family trees. Over time, and through forced interactions, we come to know our family members' personalities and learn to approach them from angles that will not cause conflict, or cause less of it. Our personal lifestyles have a huge impact on our cultural differences, including the food we like to eat and what we like to do for fun. The list goes on and on, but I think you get the idea.

Network marketing organizations can be very similar to a large, diverse family. You will need to look more closely at your family and friends when you present your business opportunity in order to find common ground upon which to stand with them. Once you determine this, you will know how to overcome the many obstacles that often cause tension in relationships. Sometimes it is easier to approach our friends than it is to talk to members of our immediate or extended family, for fear that we might somehow offend them. Using the right approach effectively guarantees that we won't receive an iota of resistance; in fact, it will be a pleasant experience. That doesn't mean they'll join your team; but they will always love you unconditionally.

There is no need to be overwhelmed by any of this, for you can learn the network marketing business in much the same way that you develop relationship skills. Of course, being shown what a lasting relationship is like and being taught how to achieve it are not the same as actually *enjoying* that relationship. In order to develop meaningful connections, we need to remember that we—and only we—are responsible for strengthening these bonds with others.

Whether it is family, friends, church, business, or community relationships you are dealing with, you need to understand that you are a person of influence. Few of us ever come to recognize how influential we truly are, and most of us underestimate the impact we have on others. But know one thing for sure: People are watching us. They are keeping their eyes open to our example, and they are aware of the attitudes we bring into each relationship. As someone once suggested, we should conduct our lives in such a manner that we would feel comfortable giving our pet parrot to the town gossip. In other words, be aware that others are always talking, watching, and listening.

Successful people work hard to develop quality relationships. If you are planning to invest your time and talents in making another person's dream or vision a reality, you want to establish a solid connection with that individual. How in the world can you start a business with someone with whom you have neither rapport nor trust? The fact of the matter is you can't. Remember, *network marketing is relationship marketing*.

One of the greatest compliments a person can receive is when a team member chooses to join your new business because you reflect the qualities that he or she admires. Relationships are important in and of themselves; and when all else falls by the wayside, it is the relationships we have built that will matter most to us. Engaged in properly, network marketing can—and *will*—result in marvelous lifelong relationships.

Every once in a while I take the time to conduct an internal review of my personal and professional relationships just to see how I'm doing. My emotional checkup consists of questions such as:

- Do I feel I'm spending enough time with those I love and care for, and want to have close to me?
- Have I cultivated all the friends and acquaintances I need to make my life complete?
- Am I satisfied with my ability to create new relationships and increase my worth to them?
- Are my relationships healthy and devoid of conflict?
- Is my circle of influence large enough; and is it possible or necessary to expand it?
- Am I on track to leave the legacy I intend?

Growing new relationships requires a kind of game plan or map. Developing these connections is like taking a road trip for which you decide beforehand how many miles you want to travel each day to reach your destination. It's the same with relationships; we must always have a clear vision of the destination we are attempting to reach with a person before we begin the journey of getting to know him or her. We should establish way points, such as phone calls, face-to-face visits, and, possibly, social events if we are to create a lasting bond with him or her. Building lasting and meaningful bonds with people takes time; they need to be tended, cultivated, and cared for consistently. I concluded long ago that genuine relationships are essential for a full and happy life.

I have also learned throughout my life that in order to form lasting, or even short-term relationships, it is critical to remove the "I" from any communication and focus on the "you." This is particularly true in network marketing. Making the other person the center of attention during a conversation is sure to get the relationship off to a great start. Listen with your eyes and heart, as well as your ears, and learn how to read between the lines.

We have all heard the saying that we have only one chance to make a good first impression. While that is absolutely true, second and third impressions are critical to relationship building, as well. Always look for the positives, and not the negatives, in your daily interactions with others.

It is human nature to gravitate toward certain individuals because we think alike or have the same interests. Occasionally, we may have so much in common with certain individuals that forming these connections seems effortless. If we consider these inherent similarities the "low-hanging fruit," then our own family members are the "fruit on the ground." We know them better than anyone, and yet we often struggle when it comes to approaching them with a business proposition. But successful networkers learn to approach everyone—including family, friends, and strangers.

One simple way to do this is to let your values guide your actions. Whether you're establishing a business relationship with a family member, friend, or fellow professional, you must explain clearly that you are both part of a team and will be building this new venture together. Remember that while products, services, and opportunities will usually sell themselves, people will join your team because they like and respect you — not merely because of what you're selling.

The days when a business could be launched on hype alone are essentially gone. Successful home-based companies are built on trust and credibility. Your relationships will determine the level of success you achieve, so always keep the lines of communication open.

We know that voicemail and e-mail are important, but there is nothing like an old-fashioned face-to-face conversation. One day, several years ago, my husband was traveling away from home and I had a few errands to run. We had recently moved to Boulder, Colorado, and that day transpired in the following way:

I went to fill the car with gas, and pulled up to the pump. After I had placed my card in the slot, the screen gave me the instructions for filling the tank and then asked if I would like a car wash. I pushed the yes button, after which it gave me my options and I selected what I wanted. After completing my gasoline transaction, I proceeded to the car wash. I drove around to the back of the gas station, where I was greeted by another automated system. I pressed the start button there and an electronic voice asked me to enter my selected code, after which I received instructions to proceed.

After the car was washed, I left and went directly to an ATM, where once again I followed the on-screen instructions. I then drove to the grocery store where I purchased a few items and proceeded to the self-scan lane; I scanned my purchases, followed the instructions on the screen readout, paid for my items, bagged them myself, and left the store.

During that entire day I spoke to no one, and no one spoke to me. I found myself asking, "Where are the humanoids?"

I relate this experience because I'm sure most of you have gone through something similar. I'm fortunate in that those days are few and far between for me; but it does beg the question, "Is this what we want life to be: talking to machines all day?" In other words, are we ready to sacrifice interpersonal contact just to save time in our busy lives?

Another example of how technology and the increasingly automated world are altering our lives is what we endure when we call an institution or organization for information. We dial the number and are automatically presented with several options from which to choose. We go through this only a few times before we learn that, often, we can bypass the options menu by punching the zero key a few times to get a "real person" on the line. Granted, these answering systems cut costs for the vendor or supplier, but if we get to the point that we never hear an actual human voice when we're seeking information, I believe life will have devolved into a sad state of affairs.

My point is you will want to partake in as many face-to-face conversations as possible when you're building a network marketing business and establishing a relationship between yourself and your contacts. At the very least, you should engage in telephone conversations with real people, not mechanized ones. It is crucial not to minimize the importance of these calls, and imperative to return any missed calls as soon as possible.

Throughout the book, we frequently refer to the difference between listening and hearing, as well as the varied ways that people listen and communicate with one another in general. It's critical to appreciate that not all communication is verbal. We are all aware by now of the advantage of learning a second language, as society becomes increasingly globalized. This trend has spurred the growth of language training systems, which can be seen in kiosks at malls, airports, and other high-traffic venues across America. However, there is one glaring omission from these language sets. I was recently in an airport and visited one of these booths to inquire about a certain language, but was unable to find it anywhere on the shelf or listed in the company catalog. I was looking for a course in "body language"—what I consider the *truly* universal language used in developing relationships. The young clerk who waited on me that day seemed a bit bewildered, but assured me that it would be coming out soon.

The most effective communication is nonverbal touching, smiling, and interacting through emotions and sentiments. The art and science of listening is a highly important tool. Ask yourself: Even if you're hearing someone else's words, are you truly listening to what he or she is saying? The so-called chemistry between humans is rarely perfect; we therefore cannot assume that because someone smiles at us and shakes our hand he or she likes us or wishes to foster a relationship with us. One huge mistake that many of us make is to assume that communication has occurred when it has not.

Most people have a lot to learn before they make their first recruiting call to a potential partner or team member. We discuss the entire process in Chapter 15, but it is important here to be aware of the potential missteps that can slow your progress and impede your success. The more diligent you are when vetting and choosing partners, the fewer pitfalls you will encounter.

Asking someone to invest time and/or money in your venture can be a daunting experience, because we often value that relationship and wish to preserve it for the long term. So proceed with caution, and do your homework beforehand. Analyze the business plan, research the product or service, and scrutinize the backgrounds of the individuals who run your company. Remember, you will be making many promises to friends based on what you know or have been told—promises often based on another person's promises to you.

Unfortunately, you won't always have positive interactions with others. I have learned that everyone has valid opinions and, like each of us, deserves the right to express them. Just because someone doesn't see your plan your way, doesn't mean that it won't work or that it's not a good idea. This is the time to leave your ego at the door and agree to move on without burning any bridges.

There will likely be a time in the future when your relationships with friends and family members will be far more valuable than anything connected to a business opportunity. My husband was always very careful in his business relationships while he was upwardly mobile in a public company; he made a point of maintaining relationships with people at all levels of the company. As he often says, "You meet the same people coming down that you met on the way up." He also emphasizes how essential it is to clearly define your destination in such circumstances; otherwise, you might reach the top of the ladder only to discover you're all alone and leaning against the wrong roof.

One of the most effective ways of enticing friends and family to inquire about your new venture is to "market" subliminally. Consider placing products you are promoting in strategic places in your home, and let houseguests or family members see you using or consuming the product. There is no risk of offending them with this strategy. After all, you need to be a user of your product, and believe in it. Seeing you consume the product will invariably inspire others to initiate conversation about it—which takes the onus off you. That's just about as nonthreatening an introduction to a product as one can get.

As I said earlier, everyone has different personalities and values, which also means that we employ various methods when forming and sustaining relationships with friends, loved ones, and business partners. These differences might depend on physical traits such as gender, strength, size, and shape, or be caused by emotional differences that reflect disposition, character, and temperament. There are also intellectual distinctions that are made by individual talents, skills, and abilities; and variations resulting from our childhood environments, during which our personalities were molded by school, friends, and home life. Our individual and social effectiveness (including sense of humor, attention to detail, and shyness or gregariousness) all fit into the equation.

All those distinctions and differences aside, there's one thing to keep top of mind no matter what your personality or preferences: Never close the door on future possibilities when approaching family and friends with a networking opportunity. And whatever you do, don't bring up the topic every time you see them—or they will stop wanting to see you!

People who are new to network marketing often ask, "What is a contact list, and how do I build one?" It's actually a fairly straightforward process: Simply take a look at the address book on your cell phone or your computer, and your friends and family lists on Facebook, Twitter, and other social media platforms. The names from these sources will constitute the start of your contact list. You will always be adding to this list; whenever you meet new people, or when others give you names of those they think may be interested in your new business venture.

Never discard old contact lists, either. Our circumstances change often and you never know when you might need or want to get back in touch with certain people in the future. I have recently begun reconnecting with some old high school friends on a variety of social networks, and am constantly amazed at the number of folks who contact me. Often they are people with whom I didn't have a close relationship in school. Nevertheless, as I age, I find myself reaching out to those I knew decades ago, and am slowly discovering that we now have more in common and are less reluctant about connecting with one another when one of us has something of value to share.

Though it can seem intimidating to make the first contact with a relative or good friend about your new business venture, the process can be relatively simple, for example a fellow networker, Albert Muir can ask, "Hey, John, is our relationship strong enough that if I wanted one hour of your time you would grant it to me as a friend?" If John says yes, your response can simply be, "Great! I can come over on Friday at 6:00 PM if that's a good time for you. Thank you. See you then."

When John asks (as he inevitably will) what it is you want to talk about, you can say, for example, "I want to discuss a start-up company that has great founders. They have already built other billion-dollar global companies. In just a very short time, this new venture has already broken all sorts of industry records, and very few people know about it. It is a potential gold mine. So, would Tuesday or Wednesday evening be better for you?"

If, however, John says, "Tell me more, or just explain it over the phone," your response could be, "John, I would love to do that, but unfortunately the material I want to share with you is highly visual and it would take hours to tell you over the phone what would take 20 minutes in person. Let me ask you a question: What is your favorite movie?" When he names one, explain how impossible it would be to describe it over the phone.

Making the movie analogy should help your friend understand the advantage of meeting personally. There's a reason people refer to our industry as a "relationship marketing" business; it's best built in the early stages by contacting friends and family members with whom you have already cultivated relationships. Establishing teams of like-minded people is just as valuable as financial wealth and the other kinds of adult "report cards."

One final thought here that can make a radical difference in earnings: Timing is *everything*. Many will decline your offer when you contact them, and it's important to keep in mind that their decision has absolutely nothing to do with you, the company, or the opportunity. In most cases, the time just isn't right for them. So wait a while and contact them in another six months to test the waters again. Never abandon your "warm" market. Eventually, those you may least expect to join may surprise you. Never underestimate your personal circle of influence.

Chapter 5

HOW WOMEN NETWORKERS GET RICH

A Venture with No Glass Ceiling

Valerie Bates

At age 18, full of dreams and lofty aspirations and feeling rich in potential, I was shaken to my core when I realized that a significant person in my life believed that there was a limit to the value that I might bring to the world. Until that sunny day in 1967 when my flight landed and I arrived home from completing my first year in college, I had assumed that my father believed in me; but on that day he announced that he would no longer fund my education— because I was a girl. I couldn't believe my ears. "Because I am a *girl?!*" I asked. Had my father told me that he couldn't support me for financial reasons, I would have understood; but this rationale was incomprehensible to me. I was shocked, dismayed, and momentarily crushed.

After I picked myself up off the ground emotionally, I resumed my education, thanks to determination, a couple of scholarships, student loans, and 12-hour days working summer jobs. I shared a tiny motel room that was en route to the university, where I cooked meals on a little hotplate and viewed everything as a brand-new adventure.

My father had inadvertently triggered many insights that shaped my character and impacted what I would ultimately accomplish as a mother, teacher, facilitator, and businesswoman. From that day forward, I took full responsibility for myself, rather than relying on others.

I hold no animosity toward Dad. I understand that his perspective on the role of women came from his background as a first-generation Irish Canadian farm boy-turned-soldier during the Second World War—that he was simply a product of his generation and environment. He served his country overseas and subsequently began a 30-year career as a mechanical supervisor, working deep underground in a rough, rugged, and isolated northern Canadian nickel mine. He made significant sacrifices to support our family, laboring year-round in mud, grease, and darkness to put food on our table. Nevertheless, my paradigm of the world order shifted *that* day—and, as a result, I have always refused to give credence to the kind of externally imposed limitations that my father expressed.

Given that pivotal experience, network marketing has always resonated with me, because there are no obligatory restrictions in our system of enterprise. Gender, ethnic background, age, race, color, and education are irrelevant. Becoming financially independent does not necessarily involve being a world-renowned researcher, spending decades on Wall Street, or fighting one's way up the ladder to the top of someone else's company. Each of us has the right to flourish as the CEO of our own business—something that is a truly equalizing opportunity.

Applying the principles laid out in this book will give you more than a fighting chance to achieve a lifestyle of freedom—regardless of gender, race, education level, or income bracket—with one stipulation: You must develop the mind-set of an entrepreneur, rather than that of an employee. With the right company, knowledge, skills, habits, and attitude, it's possible for anyone to rise to the very top. So ask yourself this question, "Why *not* me?" Think carefully about your answer, because *you* are just as worthy of wealth as any-one on this earth.

In this chapter and others you will be introduced to women who have taken control of their financial health and are earn-ing sufficient income to be classified as rich, although few would describe themselves as such. I have found that women are often unpretentious about their accomplishments, and rarely pat them-selves on the back or brag about how much money they're earn-ing. I listened with interest recently as an interviewer asked Donna Johnson, a top income earner in our profession, "What percent-age of the entire company is on your team?" and she responded, "Eighty-five percent." If he had not asked her that specific question, listeners almost certainly would not have learned about the extent of her success. Most women are simply not inclined to flaunt their income. In 2006, population aging specialist Age Wave conducted a randomized 3,000-person in-depth study on gender, money, and power. The study revealed that the security and freedom money brings is 15 to 20 times more important to women than the status and respect it affords. Perhaps that's one of the reasons that many women enjoy inclusive environments rather than individual power. We bring unique attitudes and skills to business ventures.

Yet however unassumingly these top-earning women networkers might describe their success, the fact is that many are millionaires who enjoy lifestyles of financial independence and personal free-dom. We strive for the right to be who we truly are, as opposed to the freedom to do whatever we want without consequences. Women's nature is generally (though not always) to live in harmony with neighbors and the world around us, free from both domination and subordination. True freedom allows us to live in peace.

You can rest assured that many women in network marketing are earning $1 to $2 million per year—and some far more than that. A greater number are earning $100,000 per year, while the major-ity earn just enough to breathe more easily, pay their mortgages, buy groceries, make car payments, send the kids to college, eat out, pay off their credit card debt, vacation with the family, or support charities. They are quite satisfied with that level of additional income and content to continue in their preferred activities.

REASONS WOMEN SURVIVE AND THRIVE IN NETWORKING

Although women networkers come from various career backgrounds and family circumstances, a good number of them are moms struggling to provide the basic necessities of life for their families: food, shelter, clothing, and education. As such, a few hundred dollars a month can make all the difference in the world to them.

Many successful female networkers who have pulled their families out of dire straits say that what propelled them forward was the knowledge that the status quo was no longer an option; rather, they had to accept that *they* were indeed the primary change agent responsible for improving their family's state of affairs. Having become fully aware that no one else would assume complete responsibility, they acknowledged that their children's welfare rested in *their* hands alone—and they therefore assumed leadership. Their powerful motivation compelled them to do whatever it took. This is not surprising, as most women are a positive force to be reckoned with when motivated by family matters.

Donna Imson is a wonderful example of someone who, based on her family's needs, assumed leadership and utilized network marketing to provide a quality life for her children. One night in early 1993, Donna, then a struggling young single mother of three, watched over her children while they slept and was overwhelmed by the realization that she alone was responsible for their welfare. She was a college dropout who possessed no special skills, so her earning prospects were limited. She didn't want to take a minimum-wage job and put her children in someone else's care. So, instead, she began to develop a home-based business in network marketing that would allow her to spend time with them every day. In 1998, after eight years of supporting her family as an independent business owner, Donna became a founding member of an international network marketing company based in the Pacific Rim, and has held various executive positions since. Today, she is an accomplished trainer, much sought-after public speaker, and role model for millions of aspiring entrepreneurs, especially women.

Networking offers a variety of unanticipated benefits to women, one of which is adopting a more expansive view of the world and our role in it. And once we've moved beyond survival to financial freedom, it opens up horizons and allows us to think beyond contribution to immediate family to that of a global perspective. Often, as philanthropic goals expand, retirees in networking resurface with the goal of giving more back to society.

A Chance to Give Back

My friend Debbie Campisi is one of those people. Prior to her career in network marketing, Debbie led a seizure unit in a children's hospital in Miami, where kids went for surgery to stop these life-threatening attacks. As Debbie explains, "My work was rewarding, but very difficult. Eventually, I joined a progressive networking company because it provided freedom and flexibility and allowed me to express my creativity."

After a number of years in a leading company, she was able to retire wealthy and pursue the sport she loved so much; however, she backed away from the game of tennis two years ago and made the game of networking her primary focus once again. When asked why, Debbie replied,

> I was relatively young when I retired and I feel a deep-seated need to connect, contribute, and give back. I wanted to return to building and empowering others. I wanted the challenge and everything that goes with it, including developing lasting friendships, working with like-minded, energetic people, and spending time with individuals whose values align with mine. In this profession you don't have to step on anyone's toes to get to the top. In fact, our profession often weeds out self-centered people. We rise to the top by supporting others, so it's the perfect career in which to develop lasting friendships.

Debbie's ardent desire to give back to others resulted from a defining moment when her younger sister was seriously injured in a car accident and became a quadriplegic. The tragedy changed Debbie's outlook on life, and she began to appreciate her blessings and yearn to give back. Her sister—whom Debbie describes as "a tower of strength"—taught her to carry on with grace and wisdom through whatever trials come her way. Debbie is applying these insights to her new business and has become the first woman to reach the Executive Diamond leadership level in her new endeavor.

Exodus from Corporate—Fed Up with the Glass Ceiling

A large number of women in the United States and Canada are leaving the corporate sector to establish their own companies in traditional fields and network marketing. Women in the United States are starting businesses at nearly double the national average. About 40 percent of U.S. private firms today are women-owned, compared to only 26 percent in 1997. The sales generated by female-owned organizations in the United States equal the GDP of China, Italy, or France.

Women are departing from corporations because they're fed up with bumping their heads against a glass ceiling that is deeply ingrained in capitalism. This invisible barrier allows women to see—but not attain—positions of power. In contrast, women in network marketing have an equal opportunity to go to the top. We all enjoy the same compensation plan and work our way up the success ladder without impediment—a scenario that contrasts greatly with corporate life.

In 2008, information collected by independent research organization Catalyst indicated that only 15.7 percent of Fortune 500 corporate officers were women, even though the management pool from which they were selected was slightly over 50 percent women. The percentage of female corporate officers actually decreased in 2006 and 2007, and leveled off in 2008. Women's progress in the corporate sector has been hindered, and there are few female role models at the top. The message is clear: The glass ceiling is not about to come crashing down anytime soon in the corporate world.

Authors Lynn Cronin and Howard Fine write in their book *Damned If She Does, Damned If She Doesn't,* "Women are left with two approaches for dealing with men at work: fight them or become them." It's therefore incredibly refreshing that there's no need to do either in the field of networking. Women work side-by-side with men as equals, while appreciating the differences we all bring to the table. Women's special qualities can be significant advantages in business. Network marketing offers a liberating environment for us all.

A Quality-of-Life Issue

The traditional career path of "work like crazy for 50 weeks a year for 45 years" is slowly becoming a thing of the past. Many women are leaving traditional employment because of their growing awareness of the importance of a work/life balance. Networking provides a quality of life that allows us to intertwine family life with work. It's a welcome paradigm shift, because we can build our careers around our family and lifestyle, rather than vice versa.

Katie Richter describes her life before networking in this way:

> I was burned out from politics in my education office, and the long hours, not to mention flying to various cities every month and staying in cheap hotels. When I did have time at home, I was completely drained so I basically sprawled on the couch and watched TV. The next morning, I was up at six and ready to repeat the exact same scenario.
>
> Finally, I decided that I was going to change my life. I had declined to consider network marketing for years, but I now realized that I had been denying an opportunity before even checking it out. Once I took a close look at the proposed company, I was so excited that I had trouble sleeping at night. It took some adjustments, but I made my business a priority and devoted about 10 hours a week to it. Instead of

lying in front of the TV, I connected with people wherever I was. After 24 months, my networking check was equal to my full-time income and I decided to quit my job and build my business full-time. I'm so enthusiastic about life now and am thoroughly enjoying the freedom. No more commuting, no more airplanes and cold hotel rooms, no more office politics and total exhaustion.

Other women claim that their passion for growing their own networking business stems from a desire to bring their spouse home so that they can raise their family and enjoy life together. Danelle Rich is one of those women. She recently became an independent business owner and has progressed to the Diamond level faster than any other person in her company. Though Danelle is new to networking, she's not new to business and has developed excellent business skills over the years that helped her move forward very quickly. As she says, "I want to see my husband retire in the next three to five years. He has worked so hard for our family, and nothing would bring me more joy than to see him have more time with his children, more time with me, and more time to do what he loves."

Danelle describes her and her husband's former lives as the owners of three small traditional businesses as "time bankrupt." She says, "I felt beat up by the changing economy. I began to wonder whether we would ever be able to retire or keep up with the pace required to pay the bills at the end of the month." Now she and her husband are dreaming again. "One of my dreams is to go bone fishing in the Florida Keys, fly-fishing in Montana, and salmon fishing in Alaska. Maybe I'll even splurge on some ballroom dancing lessons!" says Danelle.

It's difficult to find solid statistics regarding women's income in our profession, but it is generally suspected that although the numbers are fairly close, more men than women are top earners in many companies. Why is this the case?

One reason might be that women are more inclined to seek a greater work/life balance than men and assume more responsibilities at home. Many are less concerned about being the top earner and more worried about being an attentive mother, daughter, partner, and friend, and running the entire household. This focus has not changed much over the years for women in every sector.

Another reason may be that most networking companies are owned and operated by men. Prior to launching, companies select their team of master distributors—who are often predominantly male—to lead the field. Naturally, the masters reach out to their networks and secure their top leaders—who happen to be mostly seasoned businessmen. Women are less apt to learn about the company until men have a slight competitive advantage in terms of timing.

Though many women find ways to overcome this obstacle, wouldn't it be brilliant if owners were more strategic in their thinking and included women in the master distributor "club" from the very beginning? Think about the impact it might have if the masters recruited a balance of women and men in primary field positions right from day one. Of course, another solution would be for more women to launch and manage network marketing companies—and ensure that females participate equally from the get-go.

WOMEN BRING NATURAL TALENTS TO BUSINESS

Let's examine some of the natural talents that women bring to the business table, and how we can—and do—capitalize on them. Several of women's gifts are, in fact, double-edged swords. I realize that by discussing our aptitudes in this way I am at risk of generalizing, as women are a very diverse population group. I am well aware that each of us is unique and that one size does not fit all. However, I believe that there is some truth to the claim that females do "tend" toward certain actions, qualities, and behaviors that are valuable in our profession.

Six Natural Talents That Impact Success

Review the following traits and decide which ones relate either to you or any of the women on your team. Then ask yourself how you or your business partners could use these talents to further your business. Include this in your plan of action, and move your business forward on that basis. Keep in mind that women, just like men who make it to the top in networking, are driven and hard working, but they also possess talents that make networking a natural fit for them. In traditional business, the following traits are not necessarily recognized as key attributes for success, but they are part of the "frame" for leadership in network marketing and therefore critical to success.

Natural Talent 1: Key Leadership Attributes

Women excel in specific leadership attributes that are vital to success in network marketing. In 2008, the Pew Research Center conducted a survey and found that women shine in leadership qualities that include being "honest," "intelligent," "compassionate," "outgoing," and "creative," and were considered just as hardworking and ambitious as men. Men did rate higher in one area; they were perceived to excel at being "decisive"—in other words, more convincing.

Some women bring to networking their own self-imposed glass ceiling that keeps them from realizing their full potential. How so? Well, some simply don't step up as leaders, or decline these roles when others invite them to take them on. This is true not only in network marketing but in other sectors as well. Why do some hesitate in this way? Perhaps it's because they don't feel quite ready for the move up. Sometimes I wonder whether this is the reason so few women networkers take the lead in providing motivational and success training to our industry, and why men dominate the motivational arena. Or is it because most women are more interested in financial security than status, as the 2006 Age Wave study suggests?

A former secretary-general of the United Nations Kofi Annan was asked why there were not more women in top U.N. jobs. His reply: "I've always been interested in seeing talented colleagues move up, and in my experience, many of them are women. So, whenever an opening for a promotion was advertised, I often said to a talented person, 'You should apply for this job.' Women almost universally told me they weren't experienced enough or didn't have sufficient background. I never had a man say anything but 'Thank you, I will apply.'" Does this attitude sound like one common among the women on your team—or that you yourself express? Do you hesitate to step forward with confidence and own your power? If you want to rise to the top of our profession, you must do so.

RED FLAG

To excel in our business, others must perceive you as decisive, as this trait is generally accepted as a very important attribute of a leader. If you want people to follow you into business, you absolutely must be decisive about the value of your company, business opportunity, products compensation plan, and team. Gather your thoughts and words correctly and practice your presentation until you can deliver it confidently.

Practice, practice, practice. Start by presenting to those willing to give you feedback; and stay open to making adjustments and improving. A clear vision of your future one, two, three years down the road will help you overcome any sense of hesitancy. Chapter 8, "Deal with Yourself," provides a tool on visioning, to help you decide what's more important to you: your fear of moving forward, or achieving your goals.

Natural Talent 2: Natural Networkers

Women are innate networkers. They love to tell family, friends, and almost everyone they meet about a fabulous book, movie, newsletter, CD, DVD, TV program, website, online shopping store, or vacation deal—either to help them out or simply out of sheer delight in imparting interesting information. Sharing in this way builds a sense of community, on which women thrive.

But who, traditionally, has made all the money from enthusiastic word-of-mouth campaigns? The manufacturers and advertisers. Networking, on the other hand, *pays* us to do what we love to do. We're the marketing arm ourselves, moving products from the manufacturer to consumers through storytelling and giving recommendations. We're not "salespeople"; rather, we are educators and directors of information.

RED FLAG

Many of us might feel uncomfortable getting paid for sharing information, but that's the name of the game in our profession. Those of us who share the right information passionately to the most people—and who support others who do the same—make the most money. That's the formula for success; it's as simple as that. It involves putting our natural networking skills into a business arena.

Consider the following. Do you:

- Talk too much about your products, and assume that people are more interested in looking at them than at the entire picture of your business?
- Give a wonderful presentation, but fail to bring home results by neglecting to ask people how they see themselves fitting into the picture?
- Assume people aren't interested in the business and leave everything open-ended? People will not respect you as a business leader if you do that.

Remember to *always* confirm the next steps that your candidates want to take when you complete a presentation. This is, after all, what keeps the business moving along.

Natural Talent 3: Consummate Product Experts

Our business is ultimately focused on moving products through a distribution channel. It's therefore not surprising that many women focus on product sales rather than promoting the business opportunity. After all, we're product experts. Maddy Dychtwald, author of

Influence: How Women's Soaring Economic Power Will Transform Our World for the Better, says that women are responsible for 83 percent of consumer purchases in the United States, which translates into a purchasing power of about $5 trillion in consumer spending, an amount larger than the entire economy of Japan. Women take their purchasing responsibility seriously and make the majority of decisions regarding the purchase of new cars, vacations, food, consumer electronics, over-the-counter pharmaceuticals, health-care, and home furnishings.

RED FLAG

Women's checks will grow bigger in network marketing when they begin promoting their *entire* business opportunity. When you lead with the product and someone declines, you cannot ask, "Well, if you don't want to try my products, how would you like to distribute them?" If, instead, you ask people to take a look at your overall business opportunity and let them decide their level of involvement—either as a customer or as a business partner—you will increase the number of business partners who will help move more products through the distribution channel.

Natural Talent 4: World-Class Organizers

Women are highly competent organizers and planners—two skills that are crucial for developing a network marketing business. The downside is that some of us tend to apply these skills excessively. We are not paid to reorganize our office or spend hours planning, rather than taking, the right actions. We are paid to retail our products, recruit, and support others who do the same; *that's* where we need to spend our time.

RED FLAG

Focusing excessively on organizing can be a form of resistance to getting started, or even a form of self-sabotage. So ask yourself: "Are my organizing and planning skills moving my business forward, or stopping me? Where am I spending my time? Am I taking the *right* actions to earn a paycheck? Or am I disrupting my own success in any way?" Remember, perfectionism is a form of self-sabotage that can—and *will*—significantly stall your earning capacity. Once you are perfectly clear on your priorities, and follow the advice in this book, it will be much easier to let go of the perfectionism habit.

Natural Talent 5: Multitasking Experts
Women are known for their ability to do a million things at once.

We juggle several priorities at once because we have a multitude of responsibilities that all require attention at the same time. My daughter Christine is an excellent networker; there are times when she finds herself feeding the baby, listening to a business conference call, and cooking dinner simultaneously. During my time as a young mother with two little ones and a network marketing business, I multitasked in those three arenas in much the same way. Multitasking is a way of life for moms; unfortunately, it's not always the best way to get business done efficiently.

RED FLAG

Are you choosing your multitasking endeavors wisely? David Meyer, PhD, head of the University of Michigan's Brain,

Cognitive and Action Laboratory, speaks out against the case for multitasking. He says that it is a myth that we can operate at top speeds on multiple tasks as well as if we were doing one at a time. Splintered focus is far less effective. I suggest that you get your family cooperating and helping you with domestic responsibilities. Discuss why it's so important for them to contribute, why you're growing a business, and what success will mean for everyone. Develop an action plan together and make your family part of the solution.

Use the "law of the broom" and sweep off your schedule those activities that are not helping you achieve your intended objectives. Ask yourself where you can give up control and where you need to increase it in order to allow your business to grow. Shift some of your focus wherever possible to activities that will build your financial independence.

Natural Talent 6: Heart-Centered

Women put their hearts into their companies by encouraging team members to succeed, listening to stories of other people's struggles, and empathizing with their problems. Though these are all admirable qualities, the tendency to care so greatly for others can be a double-edged sword. Women often want others to succeed more than they want to themselves, and even can have a tendency to try to drag people across the finish line. I learned the hard way a few years into my first networking venture that people will only reach the goals they set for themselves—not the goals others set for them. Exhaustion forced me to honestly assess what was going on in my business, and I discovered that I had been doing all the work for one of my teams. When I finally handed responsibility over to them, the entire team evaporated shortly thereafter.

RED FLAG

Figure out who to support, when to support, and when to let them go. Otherwise, you'll end up with a team of co-dependents who refuse to become self-sufficient. Needy people quickly zap the energy that's required to help those who truly deserve help.

Decide on the criteria you will use to determine who to support by asking yourself the following questions: Does this team member drain my time and energy by not taking responsibility for her own actions? Is he constantly contacting me with questions when the answers are readily accessible to him (either in the back office or through customer service)? Does she miss training calls and expect me to train her privately? Does he make excuses for failing to complete his contact list? Is she actively recruiting, or letting opportunities pass her by?

If any of your team members fail to take responsibility for their business, in spite of being coached otherwise, it's safe to assume they're not committed—and it's time to move on to someone who is serious about his or her business. Always do so in a kind way; never put anyone down.

THE TOP CONCERN OF WOMEN

Recently, while having lunch with my good friend Anne, and discussing the fun and challenges of growing our businesses, I was somewhat shocked to hear her say, "It's irrational, but one of my greatest fears is that one day I'll end up pushing a shopping cart or ultimately become financially dependent on my children."

I suppose I shouldn't have been surprised by Anne's concern over economic security. Women's fears of poverty and ending up on the street run deep. Although our economic power is soaring in pockets throughout the world nowadays, we have been financially dependent for generations.

Less than 100 years ago, women in many countries, including the United States and Canada, gained the right to vote. Not so long ago, women broke through barriers to achieve basic rights like property ownership and higher education. As a Canadian, it astounds me that women in my country were defined as "nonpersons" until as late as 1929. We were officially declared "persons" that year, and therefore eligible to become members of the Senate.

Anne's concern over financial insecurity is not uncommon. In a 2006 study, Age Wave found a significant margin in responses between men and women when asked what money meant to them. By a significant margin, the men responded that it provided the *freedom* to do what they want, while two-thirds of women said *security* was the top benefit of money. Interestingly, only 10 percent of the women surveyed said they felt extremely secure. Overall, they were far less optimistic and confident than men about money. Like Anne, many women lie awake at night worrying about their financial future.

The beauty of developing the necessary knowledge and skills while building a network marketing business is that the competencies are transferable. No one can ever minimize or take that away from us. Women no longer need feel insecure due to marginalization. Networking as a profession is growing rapidly throughout the world; once we are capable of effectively building a profitable business, we will never again find ourselves at the mercy of a "big boss," a corporation that downsizes us, or one that operates unethically. There will always be a number of stellar network marketing companies inviting us to take outstanding products to the world. We are in control of our financial security—something that should relieve most women's primary concern.

HOW WOMEN CAN IMPROVE THE NETWORKING INDUSTRY

Women contribute innumerable advantages to companies—which is a good reason for involving more women at the top of network marketing companies, not just in the marketing field, but on boards and in corporate offices as well. Those corporations that include women "at the top" during the business formulation stage have a significant competitive advantage over those that don't. The bottom line is positively impacted when both women and men are represented on the board and in corporate governance.

However, we still have a long way to go. Among the top 17 publicly traded direct selling companies, only one has a woman CEO. But studies show that Fortune 500 firms with at least three women directors do considerably better in equity, sales, and working capital than those with fewer. A 2007 study by Catalyst found that those Fortune 500 companies with at least 30 percent women board members had a better return on equity by over 50 percent. Another 2007 study by consulting firm McKinsey & Company looked at 89 leading European firms and found that those with more women on the board and in senior management performed better—and actually saw their stock prices improve more.

The conclusion is simple: Diversity is the key to better performance. "Studies have shown there are different ways of approaching problems; so the more diversity you have, with regards to both skill sets and culture, the greater your chance of success," says Wendy Beecham, CEO of the Forum for Women Entrepreneurs and Executives, an association that supports women leaders.

When it becomes the norm in our profession to include at least 30 percent women on the board and in top corporate positions, the credibility of our entire profession will soar. More companies will evolve from good to great, and the number with questionable values and motives will diminish. There will simply be no room for them in the industry. At that time, a professional career in network marketing will be considered a preferable option for all ages—including very entrepreneurial young people. When this happens, we will see a significant rise in the number of financially free women in network marketing, from every age group.

It's Time to Open Every Door

The only glass ceiling in networking marketing is one that we install ourselves, whether man or woman. Women have special gifts that are germane to networking. It's not that men lack these talents; it's that women generally have them in spades and our business model values attributes such as having empathy for others while traditional business doesn't generally recognize "soft" skills as valuable business attributes.

It's a proven fact that, in terms of achievement, it's preferential to build on strengths rather than focus on overcoming weaknesses. However, strengths can quickly morph into weaknesses and hold people back in a business environment. Carefully consider how the red flags, or cautionary notes, cited in this chapter pertain to you or women on your team, and then take corrective action. If you do so while also applying what you learn throughout this book, you can achieve a lifestyle that affords a beautiful balance in family, career, finances, recreation, and contribution—the kind of life and profession toward which most serious networkers are constantly striving.

Emily Dickinson wrote, "Not knowing when the dawn will come, I open every door." This is your opportunity to open the door and step forward. Don't let it slip through your fingers.

Chapter 6

MONEY ISN'T THE ONLY ADULT REPORT CARD

Enjoying the Spirit of Abundance That Network Marketing Allows

Derek and Shelby Hall

Ever since I can remember, I have thought about what it would be like when the time came for me to retire and spend more time with Shelby. Of course, people tend to consider this fairly marginal even when they're younger; they're convinced at that age that retirement will never come. It's just human nature.

Yet here I am now, 66 years old and still not retired. Why? Because I'm enjoying the pursuit of owning my own business and watching myself and others benefit from it. I am in fact convinced now that I may *never* retire, because I've found that life can be such a joy when you have enough money to support your lifestyle but still be involved in—and contributing to—a worthy cause.

As I have aged, I have changed my definition of retirement to "doing what I want to do, *when* I want to do it!" That's my personal preference for retirement—and the network marketing model allows anyone who wants to get involved to experience exactly what I'm experiencing.

I worked for McKesson Drug Company—a venerable organization—founded in 1832—for the first 26 years of my career. I began as a part-time truck driver, at age 22, delivering drugs to pharmacies and hospitals in Ogden, Utah. The fact that I had no college education rendered my prospects for advancement unlikely, and made the obstacles seem insurmountable. However, I liked my colleagues and enjoyed our little division's culture—which meant a lot to me. So I settled in for the long haul, while hoping that something might come along that would allow me to improve my lot in life.

I was married with a child on the way at this time, and the gravity of my situation made life all that more serious for me. My greatest desire was for my wife, Shelby, to become a stay-at-home mom and be able to raise our children full-time. However, I had a long way to go before meeting this goal.

I had served a mission for my church prior to joining McKesson, and this had given me the opportunity to realize something about myself that I might otherwise not have learned. I discovered that I liked people, and that finding common ground with others was a God-given talent, one that I was able to use to my advantage. I could be very convincing at times.

The Ogden & Salt Lake City Divisions of McKesson employed about 12 sales representatives. After a few casual conversations with more than one of them I came to the conclusion that I could do every bit as well as any of them. I pressed my supervisor for an interview, and received a sales territory within a year. After five more years, I became the district sales manager in Salt Lake City.

I prospered because the culture agreed with me. I was able to attain just about any goal I set because I was allowed to. A mere four years later, I became the western regional sales manager; in four more, I was the senior vice president and chief sales officer at company headquarters in San Francisco.

Many people would consider this to be a meteoric rise to such responsibility in a (then) $10 billion company for a guy without a college education. Yet I was never asked about my absent college degree at any time during my growth in the organization. My lack of education was actually trumped by my desire to contribute to the company's success, my abundant energy, and my results.

I was a 16-year veteran of McKesson with a very bright future at this time. I was enjoying what I considered an abundant life, complete with four children, whose mother could afford to stay at home with them. But I was about to find out that the last 10 years of my McKesson career would be dramatically different than my first 16.

After a year in my role as senior vice president and chief sales officer, I began reporting to a new boss. This new boss expressed an intense need to let others know *he* was in charge; he demanded respect, even though most often he didn't deserve it. He exhibited horrific interpersonal skills, and I spent much of my time shielding my very talented staff from him. I became an insulator for them; and though they were very grateful for this, it more than took its toll on me.

At year 26 of my career at McKesson, I left to pursue other opportunities. I no longer found the job fun, and I knew that no amount of abundant living was worth the amount of aggravation per dollar.

I tell you this short personal story to illustrate that a great corporate culture, coupled with a strong desire to succeed in spite of the many obstacles that life throws at you can lead you to an abundant life, even within a corporate environment. However, it is typically reserved for the very elite. Until the year 2004, I had never seen what I considered to be "true" abundant living. That was when I took the helm of an ailing network marketing company—and took it to record highs in sales and profits in the span of just two years.

Those who travelled with me as independent business owners had never seen that sort of growth. The ones who chose to contribute and work hard enjoyed substantial personal wealth and abundant lifestyles. Many of those independent business owners are still with me today in my new venture and are once again experiencing the fruitful life that network marketing offers to all who wish to participate.

Another trait that has become obvious to me in those who join a network marketing company and work hard to succeed at it is the dearth of stress. They spend more time with their children and spouses. They go on vacations together, or take a day off when they just don't feel like picking up the phone or holding a meeting. They don't get a call from the boss; they *are* the boss!

As I pondered the aging process (and my inability to avoid it), I began to wonder when I would notice those oft-mentioned "changes" about which so many people warn. If I ever detected a subtle shift in a body function or ability, I would immediately think to myself, "Oh no, is this it?" At the same time, it seemed none of those telltale signs meant much to me. For I've decided that I would rather die at my desk doing something that allows me to make a difference, rather than clip coupons in a retirement community.

I have never actually been an independent business owner in a network marketing company. I have been a small business owner and a large business CEO. What's even more compelling is that I have seen individuals who have failed in other businesses come into network marketing and achieve wealth they never thought possible for them—or for anyone else, for that matter. There is so much that you can do once you have established your organization in a network marketing business.

A couple of years ago, Derek and I saw a movie called *The Bucket List*, starring Jack Nicholson and Morgan Freeman. It was a very humorous story of two aging men, both with terminal diseases and both with a checklist of things they wanted to accomplish before leaving this life. It occurred to us while watching that most of us do exactly what they did: wait to start on our bucket lists until it's almost too late to complete them. The reason we wait is not confined to one reason, either. We're typically too busy trying to make a living and provide for our families to even think about starting on our own bucket lists. It seems to us that we often go to work on our children's bucket lists before we focus on our own. It's a bit like the shoemaker whose kids have no shoes; other attentions and priorities take us away from what lies right in front of us. We might chip away at the list but we're never really immersed in the project of completing it because we have to get back to work, and the daily grind that comes with it.

We have both been amazed by our coauthor Mark Yarnell's stories about his paragliding passion. Mark has made over 3,000 flights from mountaintops all over the world. Though he's not exactly a spring chicken, his passion for the thrill of flight and freedom compels him to continue participating in this activity that he loves. Mark has been a networker for 20 years and has come to a point where he enjoys abundant living every day of his life. While you may not want to lift off from 10,000 feet on a paraglider, chances are that there *is* something inside you that yearns to get out into the light of day. And as Mark discovered years ago, network marketing is the vehicle that allows you to do just that.

If you are stuck in a job that will not carry you to a life of abundance—or at least to a position where you can accomplish many of the things you want to—you may want to seriously consider changing what you're currently doing. We mean *now*—not in a year or two. Seriously consider the network marketing opportunity within the next 30 days, if not this week; the opportunity is waiting for you at this very moment.

If you know someone at work, or even a relative who is in a networking company, call him or her and get started now. Your bucket list is waiting for you—and the hours and days are ticking by while you stay stuck in a job you don't enjoy.

You can let your mind run wild thinking about doing exactly what you feel like doing when you achieve this kind of abundant life. Once your organization is set and running smoothly—and you are holding your weekly training calls and your periodic three-way calls with fellow organizational leaders—the commission checks just keep growing. Sometimes you can hardly believe that you worked so hard in the beginning of your networking business for such little cash return, and now you work so little for such a huge cash return. Yet that is the very nature and beauty of network marketing.

Of course, everyone has hobbies or activities they'd "rather be doing." Unfortunately, job constraints keep many of us from getting the chance to spend much time doing them. We're so busy providing for the family and keeping our boss happy so that we don't get laid off that we delay taking some of the most rewarding actions of our lives.

Case in point: For as far back as I can remember I have loved cars—and I was so happy to learn when I married Shelby that she did as well. Together, we restored cars, we raced cars, and we just drove cars. Fifty years later I am living my dream as a race car owner and am thrilled by the action inherent in this activity. Though it's an expensive hobby, I feel secure knowing that our financial reserves allow us to enjoy something we always wanted to do. To me, that is a huge part of living abundantly.

I am also afforded the time to "give back." There are countless individuals who have a desire to serve humanity in a variety of ways—perhaps via a church mission as local as their city food bank, or as far removed as Africa or some other distant destination. The network marketing company I am currently involved with has endorsed the Habitat for Humanity campaign, which builds and provides housing to needy families all over the country. Literally thousands of independent business owners have the opportunity to participate in these worthwhile projects. And they didn't have to get permission from their boss to participate; they are "the bosses" in their organizations, and therefore gave themselves this break from work to donate their time and talents. There aren't many opportunities in the conventional business sector that offer such freedoms to those who want to get involved.

During the aftermath of the earthquake that struck Haiti in 2010, Wall Street banker, seasoned network marketer, and pilot of his own airplane A.J. Monte shuttled aid to the stricken island. A.J. had a desire to serve the people who were suffering; but if he weren't his own boss, he may not have been able to do all that he did during this critical time. I am in awe of people like A.J., who both enjoy an abundant life and choose to serve wherever they're needed to ease the burdens of others.

You can walk any path you want, at any time you want in your life. Abundant living requires that you make a consistent effort to choose healthy attitudes, set goals, and make personal commitments. Never underestimate the power of focusing on your destination as you progress along your journey. In order to do so, you have to think consistently about what brings you your greatest happiness.

Ours is our family. Derek and I are blessed to be able to take our four children and their spouses (no grandchildren on these trips) on a wonderful annual vacation. We hold a family "board meeting," during which each couple updates the others present on the activities and events in which they and their children are involved. We treasure this time spent with our children; it is one of the rewards of living with abundance.

Then, each summer, our grandchildren join us on our houseboat at Lake Powell, Utah, where we spend time with more than 30 people. It is a great time for our family to get together and celebrate life. It warms our hearts to see all the cousins interact with one another, and to hear our children discuss their own childhood experiences. Though they tease us about how we have changed the rules since the grandchildren came along, we tell them that we're just two old people doing whatever we have to do to get into heaven. I think this is the epitome of living with great abundance.

We consider it to be vitally important to do the right things in our family—and to do them for the right reasons. To that end, we have formalized a Family Mission Statement in which we have identified and agreed upon 11 key tenets, to which we as a family feel are crucial to adhere. One critical tenet is that all family members will assist in the raising of each other's children; another is to strive continually to be more Christ-like in our lives, by serving and helping others. In our opinions, this exemplifies living with abundance. Our children and extended family know what we desire for them, and are aware that we are working together for the good of all—in order to leave an inheritance for them consisting of goodwill, financial substance, and a legacy of abundant living.

As stated earlier in the chapter, residual income will allow you to have experiences many others will never know. It allows for exceptional opportunities for travel, education, continued financial growth, and, for those who apply themselves properly, untold wealth. Becoming a network marketer will allow you to achieve abundance faster than any other way we know. Your rise to abundance is a gift, to which everyone is capable of attaining. You will have much for which to be thankful—as we do. Your actions and your deeds will allow you to leave your mark on society. However, you must register your experiences and memories in your own personal life story; do not let that opportunity to leave your written legacy pass you by.

You have probably heard the old saying, "Join the Navy and see the world." I suggest changing it to, "Join network marketing and see the world." Another advantage inherent and widespread in this industry is the opportunity to travel worldwide. You can journey to conventions at least once a year, and to regional meetings anywhere from two to four times a year, depending on how many regions your organization covers. Then there are the award trips for reaching different ranks or for special promotions or accomplishments. You may have the good fortune to travel to other countries when your company chooses to enter new markets internationally. You may also get the chance to serve in a humanitarian role wherever or whenever needed.

Depending on the company you join, you may be able to invite family along, and turn business trips into vacations. Family trips can also be tacked on at the end of one of your business trips, enabling you to make it a complete family vacation. It is always a lot more fun when your family is in business with you, as then you can enjoy the conventions and award trips together.

The notion of living with abundance brings more than just a financial reward. It means working hard, playing hard, and enjoying life to the fullest. You may think that having all the money in the world will bring you abundance, but unless you have your health and your family—and a regular prescription of service to your fellow man—you will be missing out on life's greatest rewards. There must be a balance in all things.

Chapter 7

THE DISTRIBUTION MODEL OF THE FUTURE

A Fortune 500 Executive's Perspective

Derek Hall

Idiscovered network marketing after almost 40 years in the traditional retail model of distribution. I've come to appreciate it as a way one can earn a living while interacting with literally hundreds and thousands of friends, associates, and business partners around the world. It was this ability to connect with others that initially attracted me to the fastest-growing distribution model on the planet, and you can experience it for yourself.

As far as I am concerned, there is absolutely no substitution for human intervention when purchasing something—no matter what it is. Let me give you an example from my personal experience. I like to tinker with household projects, but over the years I've learned to value the knowledge of the experts when it comes to tackling larger, more difficult undertakings. Fortunately, I live about a mile from the closest Lowe's hardware superstore. I can buy just about anything there these days—from Gatorade to lightbulbs—and even grab a hot dog at the store entrance.

Whenever I visit this "home away from home" I often have with me the part(s) related to the project I'm working on that needs to be replaced. I then generally spend my first five minutes or so walking the store, reading the signs above the unending number of aisles, in the hope that, by some miracle, one of them will list the *exact* part I'm looking for. That never happens, of course, so I generally settle on an aisle that offers me hope that I'll find what I'm searching for.

Once I locate the general area where I think I might find the particular item, I begin the search. I hold the part in front of me while walking along the shelves, hoping I'll see the matching part, or even a picture of the part. If I'm lucky, I'll finally spot it. But when what I need is a bit more complicated than an extension cord or a drill bit, I know I will need human assistance to accomplish my mission.

In an effort to meet the needs of people like me who require personalized help, superstores such as Lowe's and Home Depot have now conveniently placed telephones throughout the stores, for calling a sales assistant. If I'm lucky when I do this, someone will come to my aid within a few minutes. But that doesn't necessarily mean my quest is over. For often, the employee who shows up to help me works in an entirely different department of the store and knows nothing about my problem or project; however, store rules dictate that when a customer calls, someone has to respond. Though I love the willingness of these people to assist, the next scene in my quest usually now involves *two* grown men walking down the aisle of the store holding the part in question in front of them, looking for a matching item.

The success of the network marketing model is derived from this very basic need for human interaction. We like to understand the details behind what we're buying; we want answers to questions that a fancy label on a product or a slick television commercial simply cannot provide.

Humans have always been networkers. Long before early man hung a shingle in front of his cave he was trading services and bartering goods to get what he needed in return. That could range from the deer he shot that morning to the precious piece of metal ore he dug out of the ground the day before. In either case he realized that what he owned had value to the person who didn't have it and wanted or needed it. And since it was a matter of life and death when it came to food, the accomplished hunter made money trading his prey for, say, a flint to make fire. The accomplished farmer raised crops and traded them for meat for the table or for tools to make his work easier. I think you get the picture.

Over the years, the traditional retail model has grown to monumental proportions and has become the distribution model of choice—at least in the Western Hemisphere. The costs associated with the retail model have also grown proportionately, and ultimately have burdened the consumer more than anyone else. Over the past 25 years, big-box stores and national chains began charging fees to product manufacturers and marketers. Commonly referred to as "slotting fees," they are really nothing more than rental fees assigned to the physical space on the shelf of the store where a marketing company wants to display its product. Yet despite their apparent simplicity, these fees can be enormous, as they may be assessed based on the product's size and/or the number of stock-keeping units (SKUs) required for the product. These fees are ultimately passed on to the consumer.

As retailing evolved, merchants saw a need to differentiate themselves from their competitors. To accomplish this, they began to wrap their wares in fancy boxes and other packaging, covered with brightly colored labels, all in an attempt to attract the eye of potential buyers. This marketing process—indeed, the very concept of packaging itself—became so sophisticated that today's product labels practically call out to customers from the merchants' shelves. Of course, the cost of these enhancements—coupled with the expenses incurred in the effort to capture a larger "share of wallet"—has been added to the price the consumer pays.

Then there is the advertising component, which always has enormous costs associated with it. (I read recently where 30-second advertising slots for the final episode of the *Oprah Winfrey Show* were going for $1 million per slot.) These costs are added to the final selling price, as well.

I'm sure that in reading the past few paragraphs you have noticed that what customers end up paying for the "final product"—whatever that may be—balloons dramatically according to how many marketing components are involved. It is estimated that upwards of 50 cents of every retail dollar is spent on developing beautiful and effective package and product labels, creating an accompanying and now-requisite advertising campaign, purchasing airtime or print space, and, finally, paying for shelf space in the store—the "real estate" that marketers desperately need to display their offerings to consumers.

We all recognize the value of advertising; most if not all of us have been initially attracted to a product by way of a promotion that ultimately led to our purchase of it. The effectiveness of an individual ad or ad campaign is measured by how easy it is for the consumer to recall it and relate it to the product being promoted. Nowadays, we are bombarded by messages and commercials, coming at us from all directions and all types of media—all in an attempt to draw us to products.

When it comes to costs, here too the network marketer has additional benefits. Approximately the same amount spent on product for sale in the retail model is made available to them via commissions. Moreover, most modern network marketing compensation plans offer their distributors a commission equal to or greater than the amount spent on bringing a retail product to market.

We live in a world of constant change, brought about by the Internet, smartphones, and countless other technologies. The paradigm shift in how we communicate today also affects the way we spend our hard-earned money and how we choose to allocate our time. The Internet has become a virtual treasure trove for consumers who prefer to buy products in the privacy of their home and when it's convenient for them. We no longer need to fight traffic and crowds to shop at our local grocery stores; and when we have to locate a particularly unusual item, we almost automatically go online to search for it.

There is no question that the Internet is fueling this online purchasing evolution. A growing number of us surf millions of products in the comfort and privacy of our homes; on the Internet, we can easily find the one item we need, complete with the bells and whistles we want, and at the right price. Internet sales growth is staggering; and research indicates that the growth is consistent across many industries and is outstripping the growth in the traditional brick and mortar retail stores.

This transformation in our buying habits also fuels the growth of the network marketing model throughout the world. Experts predict that this method of distribution will experience unprecedented growth and acceptance within the next 5 to 10 years, as marketers increasingly recognize the value of face-to-face selling, as compared to the huge costs of retail slotting fees, not to mention the monumental expense of advertising—which, combined, amount to billions of dollars annually, all spent on enticing consumers to buy their products.

But lower cost of entry is not the only reason I believe the networking distribution model will surpass the retail store model. As mentioned previously, there are tremendous costs associated with the "road to market" for a product; and, as also stated earlier, those costs amount to upwards of 50 cents of every retail dollar. Marketers that have products that fill a genuine need are realizing the huge edge they can have by adopting the network marketing model of distribution. They are coming to see that they can mobilize an entire volunteer army of distributors to sell what they offer—*if* their compensation plan is lucrative enough and *if* the product fills a need. The fascinating dynamic here is that the money used to incentivize this army of volunteers is the same money marketers have been paying to label developers, advertising agencies, and the large chains for space on their shelves.

Network marketing companies don't need to spend these exorbitant amounts to advertise; they use the power of the personal touch. They don't need to rent shelf space, either; they invest millions of dollars in the development of a simple selling strategy, one that all of their independent business owners can understand and duplicate over and over again.

Network marketing companies know that "real people" can effectively communicate their product message in a concise and consistent manner in hundreds of venues across the world, and that they can constantly duplicate their message to the consuming public.

I would have given anything during my years as the chief sales executive in a Fortune 500 company to have the assurance that I had a force of millions of sales reps who were consistently sharing my marketing message. This is a key advantage of the network marketing model of distribution.

While it is true that the Internet opened the floodgates to a new way of shopping and buying, we had, in fact, been seeking other ways to buy what we wanted for years. This is evidenced in the increase in catalog purchasing and the many value channels that now appear on television. I still occasionally purchase an item either from a catalog or online, but I am never completely confident that what I'm seeing in the graphic representation is what I'm going to get. And I hate getting the wrong item and then having to go through the hassle of returning it to the vendor and waiting for my credit to come through. Networking, in contrast, allows consumers to touch and feel the product *before* they spend a penny. I believe that's another very distinct and valuable difference between the networking and the catalog or online distribution models. True, some cosmetics and supplements vendors allow customers to *try* their products before they purchase; but that's about as good as it gets when it comes to achieving satisfaction. Try getting a product trial test online, from a catalog company, or from a brick-and-mortar retailer; it just won't happen (at least, not very often).

The world of "direct to consumer marketing" is exploding—and the business landscape will never be the same again. Millions of people throughout the world rely on network marketing as their primary source of income; and as a result, products are being introduced by way of this channel at an amazingly successful rate.

The Direct Marketing Association (DMA) reports that over 16 million people in the United States alone were involved in network marketing in 2010—and that number grows by hundreds of thousands each year. The DMA also cites the average annual work-from-home income for 2009 as $59,250/year, and states that 20 percent of home-based businesses grossed between $175,000 and $600,000. These are certainly encouraging statistics.

Many networkers are gaining an increased sense of security from their own home-based business. They no longer worry about losing their jobs due to recession or layoff. Rather, they are experiencing the emancipating effect of owning and controlling their own destinies and building residual income that formerly only a blessed few were able to enjoy.

Another distinction of network marketing is that it is demographically blind; it offers a nondiscriminatory route of bringing a product to market to absolutely *anyone* who has the desire for independence. I know of teenagers fresh out of high school who are using their network of friends to build their own businesses. On the other end of the age spectrum, I enjoy speaking with distributors in their eighties who are using the hundreds—and often thousands—of contacts they have made throughout their lives to begin and maintain their own companies. This makes it possible for them to improve their standard of living well into their later years, and relieve their concern of becoming a burden to their children, extended families, or the government.

Dr. Gerda Kennedy, a medical doctor and very dear friend of mine, is well into her tenth decade of life and is still an active networker. She provides income for herself and uses her personal influence among her friends and associates to maintain her lifestyle. She is striving toward a Diamond-level position at her ripe old age of 93!

I'm not saying that network marketing will bring about the demise of traditional marketing. I doubt we'll ever see the day when the traditional retail store concept will become obsolete, simply because everyone enjoys the "adventure" of shopping, the process of trying on and purchasing new clothes, or wandering through the floor displays in a furniture store. And who doesn't like to feel and smell the fresh vegetables and fruits at the local grocery store. What I am saying is that network marketing offers a viable and valuable alternative.

We have discussed the importance of choosing the right company for your own home-based business in Chapter 3. For now, it's important to review some of the financial aspects of the network marketing industry, in light of its continuing evolution.

To begin, realize that this is not your grandfather's model of multilevel marketing. Fifty years ago, distributors were required to buy product and "stage it," either in a room in their houses or, most often, their garages. Customers would come to a distributor's home to pick up their product and pay for it. The independent distributor's role was comprehensive: He was buyer, product trainer, merchandiser, and accountant; in essence, he had to fulfill just about every task required to deliver the product to the market.

Fast-forward 50 years. Today's network marketing company functions as a corporate headquarters for the millions of distributors around the world and is, in fact, quite similar to any multinational corporation. Today's network marketing corporate office provides product development, a marketing campaign, collateral materials, electronic media, accounting services, credit card processing, drop-shipping direct to the consumer, year-end tax reporting, and the countless other services that make it highly sophisticated and effective.

The retail model has developed into its present massive trade presence with help from giants like Walmart, Sears, Target, Costco, and the like. These stores attract millions of consumers, all of whom spend billions each year, while driving multimillion-dollar profits to the companies' bottom lines and providing substantial returns to corporate officers and shareholders alike. Unless you are lucky enough to be a shareholder, of course, none of this income makes its way into your pocket—except possibly by way of a reduced price during a sale.

One need not look far for examples of the success of the networking industry. Industry giants such as Amway, Avon, Mary Kay, Tupperware, Herbalife, Nu Skin, and many others have been around for decades and are proof that the model works. And since many of the largest networking companies are public companies—meaning their financial results are an open book—one can easily see that they also are financially sound. Within their own literature they report sharing upwards of 40 to 50 percent of every sales dollar with their independent business owners, while providing their products or services at very competitive prices.

Even a cursory review of the history of this industry quickly illustrates its resilience and profitability, as well as the fact that this evolving distribution model has become a viable and enduring part of the business of bringing products to market. And, yes, it's also true that the networking model has traditionally been the brunt of much criticism throughout the years, mainly due to poorly run companies operated by unscrupulous owners and investors, who, after just a few years, gutted their organizations' profitability for their own benefit and left many trusting distributors, who invested their time and money, holding the bag. I personally resent what these "slugs in suits" did to the industry I love; but I'm also proud that the industry has continued to grow and flourish thanks to the "high-ground" companies that offset the damage left behind by the "bottom feeders."

Marketing companies all around the world are drawing serious comparisons between the retail model's very expensive and ultra-competitive nature and the simplicity of the networking model. I have to believe that the Procter & Gambles, the Colgates, and the Johnson & Johnsons of the world will slowly come to the conclusion that there is a much less expensive way to bring their products and ideas to market.

As someone who has spent over 30 years working in the very competitive retail model, I say with all honesty that I wish I had discovered the networking model sooner. The focused message that an independent distributor network can deliver is so much more valuable than what can be crammed onto a product label or into a 30-second commercial. As the retail model evolves over the next 10 years, big-name companies like Procter & Gamble, Bristol-Myers Squibb, and the rest will continue to be squeezed by giants like Walmart and their ilk for higher slotting fees, advertising money, promotional allowances, and everyday low prices. And, of course, marketers will be forced to pass these growing fees along to the consumer, to protect their shrinking profit margins and their shareholder base.

Over the past 50 years, Americans and others around the world have endured more than a few economic recessions and near-depressions, when unemployment rates soared, housing values dropped, and commodity prices increased. During these periods, the population becomes extremely uneasy, which leads to even greater economic sluggishness. Notably, the networking model has flourished through these difficult times. When layoffs occur and the future looks grim, people are not just looking for a secondary source of income; they are seeking a *primary* source. In the past, the networking model has provided a safety net for those willing to invest a little to get a lot. It continues to do so today.

Economic downturns cause people to resolve that they will never again find themselves in a position where someone else controls their future. In a home-based business, you are the boss; *you* control your destiny, not some white-collar supervisor who sees you as an opportunity to reduce costs in a down economy and balance his or her departmental budget.

For all these reasons, the networking model continues to thrive. It is resilient. It is recession-proof. It enables self-sufficiency, and it empowers people. It is as American as apple pie, and it is at the core of a free enterprise system in which self-starters can make a lifestyle of choice for themselves and their loved ones. Billionaire Warren Buffet referred to network marketing as the best investment he had ever made, and *Fortune* magazine has called it the best-kept secret in business today.

Many graduating college students assume as they enter the "real world" that they want a career. They often find after a few years in that world that what they *really* want is a paycheck. The networking model provides both; but its greatest benefit is the independence and freedom that come from owning one's own business and controlling one's destiny.

The industry is attracting very influential players, from investors to celebrities, who see great opportunity for residual wealth and a handsome return on their investment. For decades, sports figures and movie stars have been lending their names to a variety of products and services. The consuming public relate readily to these well-known individuals, and are therefore drawn to the products they endorse. A growing number of these celebrity types have become aware of the networking model and the advantage they gain by applying their names and reputations to this distribution channel. The personalities who join network marketing companies pay an enrollment fee, just like everyone else; they then quickly begin receiving commissions as the organization grows rapidly, as a result of their involvement in the business venture. The icing on the cake for these celebrities is that their income continues to grow as the organization expands to other parts of the world. In time, it becomes residual income, which offers them financial security long after their names and fame have faded. I can't think of another industry that can offer this degree of security and independence.

Untold wealth is within the grasp of anyone who reads this book and becomes thoroughly engrossed in a network marketing business. And by the way, you will know when you are totally immersed when the commission check you receive is completely unrelated to what you do on a daily basis. This is when you have finally arrived at a point in your life when you love what you do because you're doing what you love.

Part II

YOUR ACCELERATION TOOLKIT—
THE FIRST 90 DAYS

Why Some Don't Make It, and
How to Be One Who Does

There are many reasons people don't make it in network marketing. Many enroll in a venture prior to conducting full due diligence on the company, as discussed in Chapter 3. Commonly, because starting a networking business requires a low investment, they don't take their decision seriously, and so fail to conduct thorough research; they move forward based on emotion, rather than on accurate information and logic. As a result, many don't anticipate they will have to face challenges similar to those in traditional business. They hear stories of individuals making big money, and all they want to do is board the gravy train, without a lot of thought. When it dawns on them that their new business is a work program, one for which they'll need to develop new skills and overcome obstacles, they quit.

Most who leave prematurely fail to understand that once they survive the potentially difficult start-up phase, the process of building a business will be thoroughly enjoyable. By then, they will have mastered basic skills, like how to invite candidates to check out their product line and business. But many people are simply not prepared to commit to developing new habits, which take time and consistent effort, so they check out of the game prematurely.

Those with fragile motivation don't last, either. Often, they aren't clear about *why* they're building a business in the first place. They've given little thought to where they see themselves in three to five years, and refuse to set goals, even though they've been told a million times that it is crucial to do so. Perhaps they've given up hope for a better life, or have little faith in themselves.

Some who quit early feel that they have little control over whether they will succeed or fail. They believe that external forces are in charge; that they are merely passive reactors to events and circumstances. They constantly play the blame game, unwilling to ever accept responsibility for their role in outcomes. Many allow their fears to defeat their chance of success.

Others leave because to stay means shifting standard beliefs about how the world works. Networking is a mind game that challenges a variety of widely accepted mental models or ways of thinking. People who implement our model must leave their comfort zone to do so, via several new paradigms discussed throughout the book. One primary concern is the "effort/reward paradigm." Most individuals are accustomed to getting paid for their efforts beginning on day one on a job. They know precisely how hard they'll have to work to earn a specific amount of money at the end of each month. This isn't the case in networking. New networkers must invest a tremendous amount of effort in their first year, or more, and often accept a return that is not commensurate with that effort. As Mark Yarnell says, "You may be the most underpaid professional around when you first start, but eventually you'll be one of the most overpaid on the planet."

Many fail to understand this "effort-to-return principle." That's why it's so important for the compensation plan to provide bonuses that are paid immediately for acquiring customers and business partners. When leaders coach new team members so that they earn paychecks early on, they are apt to stay. Never underestimate the importance of early rewards in securing loyal team members.

In this part, we focus on how to survive your first 90 days in network marketing, and to thrive beyond that. We begin by laying four foundational cornerstones for your business, to help you deal better with yourself. Next you'll learn how to develop the professional habits that drive success, and explore practical tools, competencies, and secrets that will help you develop a highly profitable business. You'll learn how to build an enormous network and support and lead your team members as they launch and relaunch their business. We also teach you how to recognize toxic people and circumstances that can destroy your career if you are unprepared. We devote the last two chapters in this part to leadership, and provide perspectives and tools to help in that regard.

The entirety of Part II is designed to help you learn about the *practical* side of building your business. It's all about skills. But reading about skills and actually using them are two different things. The only way you can really master network marketing skills is to get into the game and start playing seriously. It is our hope and prayer that what you learn in these six chapters will compel you to stay the course and, ultimately, enjoy a financially independent lifestyle. To that end, we encourage you to apply what you're learning and follow this philosophy: *I hear and I forget. I see and I remember. I do and I understand.*

Chapter 8

DEAL WITH YOURSELF

The Mentor in the Mirror

Valerie Bates

I am all that I have to work with, to play with, to suffer and to enjoy. It is not the eyes of others that I am wary of, but my own. I do not intend to let myself down more than I can possibly help, and I find that the fewer illusions I have about me or the world around me, the better company I am for myself.

—Noel Coward

Self-sabotage is one of the biggest causes of failure in network marketing—both during the first 90 days and beyond. Of course, most people don't realize that they are unconsciously ruining their own chances for success. I've never heard anyone admit during my years in this profession that they failed because they undermined their own chances of achieving their goals. But that's precisely what

91

they did in most cases. They allowed themselves to get distracted, and essentially failed to "deal with themselves."

My goal in this chapter is to help you form a rock-solid foundation that will enable you to persevere through the difficulties inherent in growing a network marketing business.

I'm sure many of you are eager to immediately get into the nitty-gritty of *how* to build a business; however, many years of experience—as well as interviews with those who have earned millions—have proven that no matter how good the systems and marketing strategies, people do not persist when their personal foundation is fragile. Without a firm sense of accountability, a powerful reason for building your business, a magnetic vision, and rock-solid beliefs, your foundation will collapse at the first sign of a storm. So I will make sure you learn about those first.

We all experience adversities, of course. The difference in how we emerge from them lies in our ability to withstand the storms and recover to higher ground each time another one hits. Newcomers who don't have the proper foundation tend to quit when faced with their first disappointment—even if it's something as simple as a potential business partner declining to join them, or receiving a shipment of products late. Most of the time, they're disappointed by something that occurs outside themselves.

Taking the time to lay your foundation does not mean that you have to get stuck in getting started. In fact, it's important to get started quickly; you should be trained and ready to go within 48 hours of having enrolled in your company. Once you have given serious attention to the tools this book provides, and gone through your company's training program, you should be ready to go.

Believe me, it is well worth your time and effort to lay a strong foundation that serves as the basis of self-motivation and personal responsibility for success. You will continue to strengthen it over time if you always remember that dealing with yourself is an ongoing, day-to-day process. Take a good look in the mirror at the person you will need to deal with—"the mentor in the mirror."

THE FOUR FOUNDATIONAL CORNERSTONES OF YOUR BUSINESS

I am often asked "What's the main reason people succeed or fail in network marketing?" My answer, without hesitation is that there really isn't *one* reason for success or failure. There are a multitude of causes; but assuming that a person has chosen a viable company, I see four cornerstones that form the foundation for success: (1) taking full responsibility for your own business, (2) having an exciting view of the future and a strong sense of purpose, (3) being sufficiently dissatisfied with the present, and (4) having a strong belief in yourself and your business. If one of those four areas is weak, it's difficult to succeed; but the good news is that each cornerstone can be developed. On the surface, networking is actually fairly simple, as the skills required to succeed in it are repetitious. But in practice it's not easy because people have to "deal with themselves" on a daily basis, as just noted. In other words, they need to look in the mirror, be honest about what they see, and make the alterations they need to succeed.

This willingness to take a good honest look at yourself before moving forward and on an on-going basis is a big part of success.

FIRST FOUNDATIONAL CORNERSTONE: YOUR LOCUS OF CONTROL

The first foundational block is the belief that each of us is totally responsible for our business. Once we accept that fact, we assume leadership and accountability for the outcomes and take control. We don't wait for anyone else to do it for us. For some, that's a hard pill to swallow.

Let's begin laying the foundation and give you a chance to look at your perception of your locus, or center, of control. Let's find out who you think is in control. Tool 1 will provide you with some insights.

Tool 1: Assess Your Locus of Control

The following is not a scientific assessment, but simply an informal means to give you a sense of your belief in your ability to create your own successful business. This tool is about appraising your locus of control.

LOCUS OF CONTROL ASSESSMENT

Please circle the response that most accurately responds to each statement by circling SA (Strongly Agree), A (Agree), D (Disagree), or SD (Strongly Disagree) to describe truthfully your feeling and/or belief today. There are no right or wrong answers; simply respond how you feel.

1.	I believe that I can choose my response to business situations.	SA	A	D	SD
2.	I believe that I can choose to move forward with courage.	SA	A	D	SD
3.	I believe that I have the power to make things happen.	SA	A	D	SD
4.	I feel that I can control my words or what I say.	SA	A	D	SD
5.	I believe that I can learn to overcome fears holding me back.	SA	A	D	SD
6.	I believe that I have no alternatives in my life.	SA	A	D	SD
7.	I believe I that I can adapt satisfactorily when life events impact my business adversely.	SA	A	D	SD
8.	I believe that setting goals increases my chance of success.	SA	A	D	SD
9.	I believe that I am responsible for my own success.	SA	A	D	SD
10.	I believe that I can change and adapt if I want to.	SA	A	D	SD
11.	I like my profession in networking.	SA	A	D	SD
12.	I believe that my past dictates my potential.	SA	A	D	SD
13.	I am open to taking risks.	SA	A	D	SD
14.	I believe that my attitude affects my level of success.	SA	A	D	SD
15.	I feel at peace most of the time.	SA	A	D	SD

16.	I am aware of how my self-talk impacts my success.	SA	A	D	SD
17.	I believe I can cultivate the right thoughts if I want to.	SA	A	D	SD
18.	I believe that success in networking depends on my leader.	SA	A	D	SD
19.	I am open to new ideas and perspectives.	SA	A	D	SD
20.	I am happy with my personal life.	SA	A	D	SD
21.	I am open to using visualization as a tool for business growth.	SA	A	D	SD
22.	I surround myself with people who support my personal growth.	SA	A	D	SD
23.	I surround myself with those who support my professional growth.	SA	A	D	SD
24.	I believe that I can expand my horizons as far as I can imagine.	SA	A	D	SD
25.	I believe that I can change my habits to produce better results.	SA	A	D	SD

All items (with the exception of 6, 12, and 18) that you marked Strongly Agree indicate a high *internal* center of control—a belief that *you* are in control and responsible for your own success. Likewise, items 6, 12 and 18 that you marked Strongly Disagree show a high internal locus or center of control.

Take a look at those items you assessed otherwise. Those answers point toward a tendency to attribute success or failure to outside forces—in other words, toward an external locus of control.

If this assessment reveals that you have a predisposition to attribute results to outside forces, take a closer look at why you evaluated yourself as you did. Can you think of specific instances or situations in which you've surrendered accountability? Do you do this often? What have you found to be the ramifications of doing so? Begin working on your beliefs in order to understand where these perceptions are coming from. Then decide how you will proceed to change this perspective. Keep looking to the mentor in the mirror for answers.

Many new independent business owners let themselves down early in the game; and they won't admit that it's because they don't believe in their power to produce results. Instead, they claim that the company, products, and/or their team leaders have let them down. They quit and join the next "latest and greatest" venture, only to quit again and attribute this new failure to external forces as well. Their pattern of failure is based on a refusal to accept personal responsibility for both their choices and their response to circumstances.

SECOND FOUNDATIONAL CORNERSTONE: YOUR PURPOSE AND VISION

I can think of few professions other than networking where purpose and vision—variables over which each of us has complete control—play such a vital role in success. I'm referring to purpose and vision that come from deeply held beliefs about what is possible in your life. To achieve your purpose and vision often requires that you step out of your current comfort zone and decisively design your own life without limitations. The tools that follow will help you establish your second cornerstone for success.

Tool 2: Clarify Your Purpose

Purpose is critical; we are powered by emotion, and not necessarily by reason. That may come as a surprise to pragmatists who are under the impression that we make rational decisions most of the time. On the contrary, a growing body of evidence shows that emotion is in the driver's seat. Donald Calne, neurologist and author of *Within Reason: Rationality and Human Behavior*, points out that the essential difference between emotion and reason is that emotion leads to action, while reason leads to conclusion. Never underestimate the power of purpose—the desire to make a difference—in driving you forward in your business.

You can establish this building block by clarifying what's compelling you to build a network marketing business. Set aside some quiet time to think, unearth, and record *all the reasons that your business* is important to you. Getting clear on this will help you stay the course through thick and thin, so think carefully about what you value most. Some examples might be: having time with your kids, quitting your job, establishing a community of people who share certain values, going on vacations, or making life more financially comfortable.

The reasons are immediately obvious for some, like the women profiled in Chapter 5 who are passionate about providing a good life for their children. Others, however, need to explore beyond the surface to reveal their underlying driving force. If that's the case, and you want to dig a little deeper, select your initial reason for building a business. It might be "more money." Ask yourself: "Why is that so important to me?" Once you've answered that, ask a follow-up question: "Why?" Keep doing so until you've asked why up to five times and you'll get to the heart of what will inspire you to move forward with passion.

Here's an example of how this tool works. Let's say that you've identified money as your driver.

Ask first why: Why do I want money?
Answer: So I can invest in retirement.

Ask second why: Why do I want to invest in retirement?
Answer: So I don't have to worry about living in poverty in my later years.

Ask third why: Why am I concerned about that?
Answer: Because I don't want to be dependent on anyone.

Ask fourth why: Why don't you want to be dependent?
Answer: Because I'm very independent and want to remain that way for the rest of my life.

Ask fifth why: Why do you want to remain independent?
Answer: Because I want to always live in dignity.

On the surface, money seemed to be your purpose for building a business, but below the surface the true motivation is to live in dignity. That insight changes your personal story to one that has greater meaning than simply the desire for more money and having a passionate reason for building your business will drive your motivation.

Tool 3: Craft Your Vision and Embed It into Your Subconscious

Before you craft your vision, first consider beliefs you may have about your life, and in particular about your business, that might hold you back. Answer the following questions: What beliefs do you hold about your business? Do they propel you closer to your professional goals, or push you away? Select one goal—perhaps a promotion level or monthly income—that you want to accomplish right away. What timelines, methods, and people have you locked on to? What options have you locked out? Are there other ways? What other locked-on/locked-out perspectives do you need to change in order to grow? Now, what *new* beliefs do you want to lock in? The answers to these questions will prepare you to write a more exciting vision of what is possible, and that will fire up your passion.

Once you've expanded your thoughts about what is possible, write a vision of your life one to three years from today's date. You want your vision to compel you to move forward with unstoppable passion. Sit down in a quiet place, where you will not be interrupted, and allow yourself to dream—perhaps for the first time in years. Imagine the following celebration in as much detail as possible; include a clear view of your business, finances, physical health, mental health, spiritual health, relationships, learning, and recreation:

> You've gathered together with team members, family, and friends to celebrate your successes over these past one to three years. You have achieved outstanding goals in your business and personal life. Imagine the high spirits!
>
> Why is everyone celebrating? What have you accomplished? What does your life look like now? What does your business look like? Who is with you? What are they saying?

Take the time right now to write your vision. (Some people will also enjoy creating a vision board on which they post photos.) Write a story of the celebration in the present tense ("I have . . . ," "We are . . .") as if you have already accomplished all you are describing. Choose a vision date three to four years out from now. Many people find it easier to begin with the following statement: "It is now [the date three to four years from now] and we are celebrating because . . ."

Use Imagery to Make Your Vision Come Alive

Now that you have crafted your vision, the next step is to envision the future in such crystal-clear detail that you can see your new life, or new "reality," and feel the emotions that accompany it. Post your vision—either in writing or photos and drawings on a vision board—where you can view it several times a day. Each time you study it, allow yourself to feel the emotions that accompany it— such as satisfaction, peace, excitement, confidence, and joy.

The reason for doing this is because the subconscious mind does not distinguish between an experience that is real and one that is imagined with great clarity and emotion and we are so drawn toward that which we focus on that the roadblocks along the way don't register as major obstacles. This concept is not new; top athletes and performers consistently use visioning, imagery, or mental rehearsal to improve their performance. As they practice, they "see" themselves in their mind's eye performing perfectly, and their performance follows suit. Visualization will help to embed your vision in the same way. I have used affirmations for years to assimilate a preferred reality or vision—and they've worked amazingly well.

THIRD FOUNDATIONAL CORNERSTONE: YOUR HONEST ASSESSMENT OF CURRENT REALITY

An honest assessment of where you are today relative to your future is one of the cornerstones of motivation, for without an honest evaluation of your current reality, nothing much will change. It's acknowledgment of the gap between your vision and current life that will create the drive or tension to move you forward. Use the following tool to assess your current reality.

Tool 4: Assess Your Current Reality

You based your vision on eight interrelated components of your life: business, finances, physical health, mental health, spiritual health, relationships, learning, and recreation. Now, assess your current reality in each of those same eight components. Write down your current reality assessment. The biggest challenge in cementing this cornerstone and making it work for you, is moving out of denial and telling yourself the real truth about your current state of affairs. Do your best to not gloss over the way "things really are today."

Talk it over with a partner and then commit to moving forward. Set goals, based on closing the gap between your current reality and your ideal vision and then go for it. You will have plenty of means of moving forward with greater confidence when you have completed this book.

Mark Yarnell's own story of why he joined a network marketing company, how he adopted a new vision of what was possible, and how he conducted an honest reality check on his current state of affairs provides an excellent example of the way the four corner-stones create motivation that results in massive action:

> In April of 1986, the board president of my church—a man named Bill—showed up at my door with an interesting good news/bad news scenario. I had served as his minister for a few years; the Texas economy was in bad shape, and our biggest contributors were filing for bankruptcy. The bad news was that my salary was being cut again. The good news was that Bill had an exciting ground-floor opportunity to show me.
>
> When I learned that it was network marketing I thanked him politely, but declined to participate. He left me with a photocopy of a $57,000 check, which he claimed his team leader had earned the previous month. As I sat looking at that check, a number of ideas began to surface. They had very little, if anything, to do with my current reality. I never expected to earn big money as a minister, so I accepted my condition as "normal." However, what really struck me as I continued to glance at the silly check copy was what I could accomplish as a *rich* minister.

For a couple of days, I allowed my mind to wander through all the possibilities of a life of wealth. But it would be disingenuous to pretend that I was solely motivated by altruism. For nearly a decade, I had few challenging thrills in life. People came to see me because I was their minister. I spoke twice each week to appreciative parishioners. They loved me, I loved them; there were few challenges.

At age 36, my life had become routine and predictable. My friends were members of the same families who were my parishioners. They respected me, and I cared deeply for them, but I followed an important rule: Never try to build an open relationship with individuals who expect you to act like God's spokesperson. That's not an open relationship.

For two days, I continued to think about the $57,000 check, imagining what I could do with that kind of money. I concluded that I really needed a new challenge—one that would allow me to make a greater difference. I wanted to start with having more fun and building a new community of friends who liked me for who I was, rather than for what I signified. And you know what? I'll admit it; I really *did* have a secret desire to see if I could become rich.

After mulling over the possibility for a number of days, I called Bill, invited him to my house, and enrolled in the company. I used the money I borrowed from another member of my church. That's when—and how—my network marketing adventure began.

Mark went to work immediately, operating more on passion than knowledge. He was willing to do whatever it took to succeed. Four years later, he received The American Dream Award from The Ruff Company for his hard work and creativity in turning an opportunity into success, thereby exemplifying the American dream. He had gone from life as an impoverished minister to living a life of relative wealth; he acquired numerous lifelong friends, who appreciate him for who he really is; he has weathered many storms—and has had a ton of fun in the process.

The next cornerstone will provide the final foundational block for your business.

FOURTH FOUNDATIONAL CORNERSTONE: YOUR BELIEF

Tool 5: Engage the Power of Belief

It's next to impossible to succeed without rock-solid belief in yourself and your vision; the industry or profession; and your company, products, and pay plan. That's why I consider belief a foundational cornerstone to your success.

How solid is your confidence in each of these critical areas? To find out, complete the Belief Assessment tool provided here. By doing so you will gain insight into where you need to close gaps by strengthening your beliefs—and therefore your confidence. Remember, becoming more aware of areas to improve will help you in building a more profitable business.

You can build a solid foundation for your business by implementing the tools in this chapter, and you can enhance your belief by actually building your business. Nothing happens when you sit on the sidelines as a spectator. This is a hands-on endeavor; you've got to get in the game. As you take action more and more, everything grows—confidence, belief, passion, and the size of your check.

BELIEF ASSESSMENT

Consider your confidence level in each of the following key areas. Then, on a scale of 1 to 10, indicate your responses.

a. Belief in yourself

1   2   3   4   5   6   7   8   9   10

Rock Bottom _____ Rock Solid

Key Solution: Practice builds confidence; step forward and take action (see Chapters 8, 9, and 10).

b. Belief in your vision

1   2   3   4   5   6   7   8   9   10

Rock Bottom _____Rock Solid

Key Solution: Post your vision in a visible place and review it daily. Use affirmations.

c. Belief in the network marketing business model or profession

1   2   3   4   5   6   7   8   9   10

Rock Bottom _____Rock Solid

Key Solution: Name at least three reasons why this is a viable model (see Chapters 1, 7).

d. Belief in your company

1   2   3   4   5   6   7   8   9   10

Rock Bottom _____Rock Solid

Key Solution: Evaluate your company (see Chapter 3). Stay engaged through training calls, meetings, and conferences.

e. Belief in your products

1   2   3   4   5   6   7   8   9   10

Rock Bottom _____Rock Solid

Key Solution: Fall in love with your products by using them daily; collect testimonials from others who use them.

f. Belief in your compensation plan

1   2   3   4   5   6   7   8   9   10

Rock Bottom _____Rock Solid

Key Solution: Take the right actions to earn a check as quickly as possible, based on your pay plan and help your team members do the same.

Chapter 9

PRACTICE THE PROFESSIONAL HABITS THAT DRIVE SUCCESS

Valerie Bates

Metaphors are excellent tools for gaining perspective. For that reason, my husband Mark Yarnell and I occasionally compare our business challenges to the Greek mythological King Sisyphus, endlessly rolling a heavy boulder up a steep hill. The image of pushing to the top helps give us a fresh perspective; it compels us to regroup and recommit to stay the course. Mark and I often remind ourselves that struggles are simply part of achieving anything significant. We think about our love of the challenge, the income potential, the special contribution we want to make worldwide, the difference we're making in people's lives right now, our responsibilities as leaders, and we're reinvigorated. It doesn't take long, just a matter of minutes, to refire on all cylinders by invoking the Sisyphus metaphor.

You can find cartoon video clips of Sisyphus on the Internet. Problem is, we've never actually seen Sisyphus topple the boulder over the hill so that it rolls down the other side under its own momentum in those clips. Yet in networking, by perfecting the professional habits described in this chapter, you can push your boulder over the top. It's done every day in networking.

To generate the force necessary to budge the boulder (your business) from a stationary position into a rolling motion, you must exert all of your power and direct your focus consistently. Sometimes the boulder rolls backward just as you are making progress; it is often on unpredictable ground and so moves a few feet forward only to inch back again. Through practice, though, you eventually get the hang of pushing it up the hill. You develop the skills you need to anticipate and, thereby avoid, the bumps that set you back. You learn to leverage your strengths and — accompanied by a like-minded team — you finally are able to push the boulder to the very top of the hill. At the fulcrum, the *tipping point*, it takes only a nudge to send it down the other side of the hill. At this point, even if you *wanted* to stop it, you couldn't. It's "in momentum." Thanks to the right focus, skills, habits, and team, the boulder rolls freely down the smooth slope on the other side.

In a recent work entitled *The Lotus Code*, Mark Yarnell and I provided a system for achieving accelerated prosperity; we showed how developing the right thoughts, words, and actions results in habits that act as a tipping point on a success system. At the habit level, networking ceases to be a struggle and — for the most part — becomes a joy as your business slips into its own momentum, based on the right habits.

THE SIX HABITS OF PROFESSIONALS

This chapter highlights the six most important habits that drive success. Rich networkers hold the key to developing habits faster. They don't practice harder, or even much harder; they practice much, much, *much* harder!

People build habits by combining live practice with mental rehearsal or visualization. As explained in Chapter 8, this kind of imaging works because the human brain does not differentiate between events or actions that are vividly imagined and those that are actually experienced. Top networkers assimilate habits both literally and in their imagination.

Although the first 90 days in business can prove challenging, everything becomes easier once the *right* habits are entrenched.

Generally, it takes 21 days to embed new habits; however, professional networking habits often take 90 days, because they are multifaceted. This is why it's especially important that you constantly evaluate your progress and identify any actions that you need to fine-tune and reinforce.

You may wonder as you review these professional habits which are the most crucial to develop, and how many you should work on simultaneously. The answer is that it's impossible to assess the hierarchy of importance here, for all of these habits work together synergistically to drive success. Forming one habit often triggers a domino effect that prompts others to fall into place almost naturally.

Habit 1: Creating Dreams and Goals

Most networkers set goals initially but fail to realize how vital it is to make dreaming and goal-setting a *regular* habit. Success begins when you keep the end in mind constantly; so start your journey by identifying any self-imposed limitations and allowing yourself to dream big. As recommended in Chapter 8, "Deal with Yourself: The Mentor in the Mirror," create a vision and clarify your purpose, or "why." It's as simple as that. Rich networkers bounce back easily from temporary setbacks because they focus on those two bigger perspectives; poor networkers focus on the bumps in the road.

Crystalizing the future is not a one-shot-wonder event. It's organic and free-flowing, and you must make a habit of revisioning and re-creating goals if you want to succeed. Most people start with survival goals; but once they witness others succeeding, and then taste success themselves, often they lift former self-imposed limitations and stretch their vision further. Whenever passion begins to wane, reinvigorate yourself by revisiting your ambitions; ask yourself why you set them, and, if necessary, set new goals that excite you. I've often witnessed loss of motivation over the years from those who don't goal-set through to the next level after they reach a current goal. They settle prematurely into a comfort zone and allow their checks to plummet. They haven't yet developed the *habit* of dreaming, revisioning, and setting new goals.

There is no need to stagnate; goalposts are erected by the very nature of our business, in the form of financial goals, leadership and recognition levels, bonuses, percentages of market shares, size of team, and number of people attending meetings or conventions. What goals have you documented for this month and the next 90 days? Use the launch and relaunch tool in Chapter 10 to accomplish this. Have you made it a *habit* to dream and reset goals?

Habit 2: Cultivating the Right Thoughts

The reason that habitually thinking the right thoughts is critical for driving success is simple: Thoughts are the first step on the success continuum; *everything* begins with thoughts. So when we develop the right kinds of thoughts—those that support our vision—all else falls into place. The challenge we face is that launching a new business often triggers self-defeating thoughts. Our inner critic, our self-talk, insists that this new venture will not work, for a variety of reasons. It is intolerant of ambiguity, loss of status quo, or risk.

Viewing our inner critic as the "Monkey Mind" is helpful in understanding this phenomenon. This term, from Eastern philosophy, represents a state of mind that jumps from thought to thought like a monkey jumps from tree to tree. Monkey Mind engages in passing thoughts, always chattering, expressing doubts, complaining, making excuses, defending, blaming, and initiating fear. The further we venture into the unknown journey that a new business presents, the more insistent Monkey Mind becomes. Negative thoughts snowball, and the snowball is soon rolling downhill, growing and gaining momentum. This is precisely what causes people to quit in the early stages of network marketing and go back to their comfort zones. They don't know how to deal with Monkey Mind.

But there is a way for you and your team to immunize yourselves against such defeating thoughts. Dr. Jonas Salk, the scientist who discovered the polio vaccine, once told Dr. Martin Seligman, author of *Learned Optimism: How to Change Your Mind and Your Life*, that if he were a young scientist today, he would focus on immunizing kids *psychologically*. That idea resonated with Seligman, inspiring him to conduct three decades of research with hundreds of thousands of adults and children. He concluded that mastery of three thinking skills builds confidence and optimism:

First, observe and catch your thoughts.
Second, evaluate the accuracy of your thoughts.
Third, reframe your thoughts more accurately.

Let's look at a practical example of how, using this process, you can redirect or cultivate thoughts so that they are empowering, rather than disabling. An initial thought might be, "I'm a lousy recruiter and will never get anywhere in this business." Noticing and becoming aware of that thought is step 1. Next, you evaluate its accuracy by asking, "Is that really true?" Finally, you correct it by concluding, "That's not completely true. I'm not the best recruiter right now; but I'll improve if I keep practicing." The process is not complicated; it just requires that you practice in order to make healthy thinking a habit.

Once you become proficient, you can habitually nip negative thoughts in the bud. Neuroanatomist Dr. Jill Bolte Taylor, author of *My Stroke of Insight*, talks about the importance of doing just that. She calls it "tending our garden," and states,

Regardless of the garden I have inherited, once I consciously take over the responsibility of tending my mind, I choose to nurture those circuits that I want to grow and consciously prune back those I prefer to live without. Although it is easier for me to nip a weed when it is just a sprouting bud, with determination and perseverance, even the gnarliest of vines, when deprived of fuel, will eventually lose its strength and fall to the side.

So when you fear rejection or have doubts about yourself and your ability, choose to consciously "tend your mind." Stay resilient by making it a daily *habit* to monitor your self-talk and become aware of self-defeating, disempowering thoughts; and then cultivate them for better results. You'll be delighted with the sense of power and confidence you experience when you assume the authority to nurture your own thoughts. And the astounding benefits will extend to every area of your life.

There is a strong correlation between self-talk and how you view your potential. How do you rate your self-talk regarding your business today on a scale of 1 to 10—with 1 being negative and 10 being positive? One way to increase awareness of your thoughts is to write them in a daily journal, review them, and look for defeating patterns. Then, using Dr. Seligman's formula, prune back the unhelpful ones. If you use this process to stay enthusiastic, others will want to join your team. They'll notice immediately that you are genuinely happy, having fun, and making plenty of money.

Habit 3: Renewing Your Spirit

Were you to shadow networkers who excel in business, you'd notice that they exude energy, are enthusiastic, and have confidence in where they are going and the value they bring. Their posture is strong; they're always "on" when engaged in business. Even if they have made the same presentation a hundred or more times, you might assume from their demeanor that the current one is the most exciting they've ever done. They love what they do, find it meaningful, and are totally focused on the present when prospecting or presenting. In short, they are "all-in."

Perhaps you're wondering whether this optimism comes naturally or they've learned it. The truth is that most of them had doubts and concerns at first, but set themselves up for success by developing the habit of renewing their spirit daily through healthy thoughts, interesting ideas, supportive people, and a zest for achieving. They are purpose-driven and laser-focused on where they are going.

While many are too busy to set aside an hour a day for personal development, they make a habit of integrating learning and motivation as they go about daily living. Some of their renewal activities or tools include:

- Watching motivational videos.
- Listening to CDs while driving or exercising.
- Studying the lives of inspirational mentors.
- Subscribing to daily inspirational quotes.
- Praying or meditating.
- Spending time contributing to a favorite cause.
- Savoring nature.
- Acknowledging and appreciating blessings each day.
- Telling at least one person each day how special he or she is.
- Learning something new every day.

Why not commit right now to forming one or more of these renewal habits yourself? Select your favorite methods and work them into your daily schedule. Top-notch networkers find ways to make themselves and others feel good about life. They're always dreaming, learning, aspiring, and inspiring those around them. Rather than zapping other people's energy, great networkers breathe energy into others. They are attractive to others because they are in the *habit* of renewing their spirit.

Habit 4: Letting Go of Rejections

In Chapter 15, Mark provides a healthy perspective on rejection and outlines several rejection-free marketing strategies. It's wonderful to find people who are receptive to an opportunity through using these strategies, but ultimately, every successful networker must develop the habit of letting go of rejection in order to persevere long term. When we take the focus off ourselves, empathize with others, and focus on what we can do for them, the very idea of rejection takes a back seat. The focus moves from "me" to "you."

Those with a healthy internal center of control will find it relatively easy to let go of rejection because they are confident they can manage how they respond to situations. They don't take rejection personally or become disheartened when someone fails to consider their business or declines during the due diligence process.

In contrast to those who feel dejected, they don't carry the response as baggage to weigh them down.

Effective networkers make it a habit to let go of rejection. To begin with, they practice inviting others to check out their business or products and become skilled at making others feel at ease. These aren't skills they achieve overnight; they develop them through practice. Aside from having facile "inviting" skills and using rejection-free marketing strategies, every successful networker must have a healthy perspective on rejection.

One of the best defenses against being waylaid by rejection is to assume that a candidate who declines is simply not in a "change window" at this point in his or her life. At both times in my life that I entered networking I was dissatisfied and looking for a solution to my problems. The first time, I was at home with two small children and wanted to improve family finances so that I could continue to be a stay-at-home mom. Twelve years ago, when I entered networking for the second time, I was going through a divorce and wanted to secure my financial independence through earning residual income in an open-ended opportunity. The point is, I was open to change in both cases.

Most of the time, people decline to join our business because the timing is not right; nevertheless, new networkers often struggle with accepting that rationale. Please note that this kind of reasoning is not an excuse for developing subpar skills at inviting people to investigate your business and products. It's up to *you* to work with your team leader to practice and develop good skills. That's a given. The Four-Room Apartment model that follows will help you better understand the importance of the "change window" as it relates to rejection and show you how to adopt a healthy perspective.

The Four-Room Apartment Model

Swedish social psychologist Claes Janssen developed a theory that likens change to living in a four-room apartment. Throughout our lifetime, we all move through four predictable stages that can be represented by rooms in an apartment (see Figure 9.1). Think about this from a prospecting perspective:

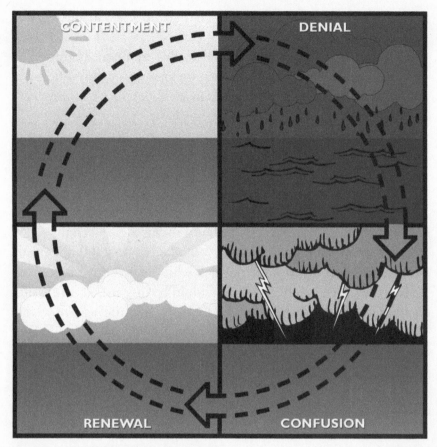

Figure 9.1   The Four-Room Apartment
Source: Heather Symes

Room One: Contentment. People living in this room are
content; they are not looking for options. They don't want
to change because the status quo or comfort zone feels so
good. No matter how skilled your invitation or presentation
to these individuals, they will *not* join you, so you need to let
go and move on—without feeling rejected.

Room Two: Denial. People in this room have intimations of
discontentment with the present, but are not yet prepared to
face it and so remain in denial, for a variety of reasons. They
may realize unconsciously that when they do face their current reality, they will enter the confusion room (Room Three)

and have fears about doing so. They are *not* open to looking at a business opportunity.

Room Three: Confusion. Those in this room are confused; they are seeking answers and are open to possibilities—which means they *may* be open to checking out business options.

Room Four: Renewal. This is where people eventually give up what they've been hanging onto in the confusion room and move forward into renewal. They're at a turning point and *may* be open to your invitation.

People in the confusion and renewal rooms are in a change window. The problem is that we network marketers are standing outside the apartment and can have no idea which room any one person is occupying. Some look like they should be dissatisfied, while others look like they are contented. However, because we know very little about their lives, we may be mistaken. Simply put, we often have no idea which room they're "living" in. All the more reason to adopt the habit of letting go of rejection and assume there's a good chance that the people who decline our invitation are simply not in the right room at this time.

Don't take their rejection personally; it's not *your* issue, or your job to change their perspective. This is *their* life; wish them well and move on. But save their contact information, and get in touch with them later—because you never know which room they'll be in six months from now.

Habit 5: Having Courage

The habit of courage in networking involves the practice of remaining steady while facing challenges on a daily basis. To me, Nelson Mandela personifies courage. He sees courage as the way we *choose* to *be*: it is all about how we react to different situations. He says that it is in stepping forward and *pretending* to be brave that we become courageous. That is precisely what Mandela did throughout his 27-year imprisonment.

In networking, this perspective on courage may translate into the willingness to break life-draining patterns or habits of thought and action. It may involve how we respond to rejection, how we proceed in faith when business results are dismal, how we withstand naysayers, how we deal with looking less than "professional" while practicing new skills, how we have compassion and accept others just as they are rather than judging them, and the courage to break free from habits that are no longer serving us while adopting new ones that will carry us forward to a better life.

Growing a large business requires you to take consistent action, yet "getting stuck getting started" is a typical problem in networking. People often postpone getting into the game for so long that their motivation dwindles and they quietly fade away. Their procrastination is often prompted by a variety of fears, including a diminishing reputation, looking unprofessional while climbing the learning curve, having to learn new skills, losing face with family and friends, earning too much money, not having enough time, being embarrassed, and on and on.

How *do* we move forward in the face of fear? One way is to, "Just Do It," pretend that we have courage and move forward. We can also minimize fear by ensuring that several factors are in place, and we can use a tool called Gleicher's Formula for Change to get an idea of what to do next to move our businesses forward. The formula is:

$$V \times D \times F > R$$

where:

V = Vision of what is possible
D = Dissatisfaction with the present
F = First steps forward
> = Is greater than . . .
R = Resistance (fear)

Thus, Vision times Dissatisfaction times First Steps must be greater than Resistance or Fear. Because V, D, and F are multiplied, change will be low if any one of these elements is low or absent, thereby rendering us incapable of overcoming the resistance.

Now figure it out for yourself: Which factors do you need to strengthen in order to succeed? Though this book offers perspectives and provides strategies for overcoming fear and building belief and confidence, when it comes right down to it, nothing will happen until you step forward and take action. Courage is the key.

Contrary to popular belief, courage is not the absence of fear; rather, it is the willingness to step forward in the face of fear and not let being afraid stop us from doing what we want to do. This very act builds confidence; and if we do it often enough, courage becomes a habit. This is precisely why we admire new networkers who step forward and stretch outside of their comfort zones.

Amber and Dean's Story of Courage

For the past couple of years, Mark and I have worked with a young Canadian couple out of Vancouver, British Columbia, that we admire a great deal. Amber and Dean De Grasse are an inspirational team who relentlessly demonstrate courage. Dean was on the street at a very early age, developed street smarts, and essentially raised himself. That took courage and Amber is full of zest for life and never backs away from a professional challenge. They're dynamic and relentless recruiters. Both left highly successful, 14-year careers in real estate development in order to build their network marketing business. They were highly motivated to do so by the promise of a lifestyle of freedom and adventure.

Like many professionals, their biggest challenge when getting started was making the adjustment from proficient professionals to fledgling networkers. As Amber explains, "We couldn't walk and chew gum at the same time in networking. It was embarrassing, especially within our 'warm' market, but we kept practicing and eventually got good at prospecting and presenting the business." Of the multitude of interesting stories they delight in telling about the trials and tribulations of growing accustomed to their new career, the following tops the charts:

We had just signed on a new business partner Scott who organized his first private business reception on a Wednesday evening in his home. Guests responded positively to his invitation and 12 people had reconfirmed attendance the prior day.

Amber and Dean went on to explain that only two guests had arrived by start time, including a young man in uniform and Scott's girlfriend (who wasn't interested in the business, but had come to support her boyfriend). Ten minutes later, when no one else had appeared, the host began calling everyone who had accepted his invitation to find out where they were. Some answered their cells and professed surprise that this was the meeting night. Scott's mom called to say that she couldn't make it, as she was having chest pains and was on her way to the emergency room. Two more family members and their spouses said they were going to the hospital to support the host's mom. And when the host reached the last two people on the list, initially they said they were on their way but changed their minds after learning about his mother and decided to head to the hospital, too. At that point, Scott excused himself to "go to the bathroom," then Amber and Dean watched in dismay as he drove out of the driveway. This whole incident transpired within just a few minutes.

Dean recalls:

> We were mystified, but still committed to doing a presentation, so we explained our business to the young man, who promptly signed up and bought a business kit. We had captured victory out of the jaws of defeat!
>
> The following week, the new independent business owner set up his own private business reception, and 15 people confirmed. On meeting night, we enthusiastically headed off to the meeting. Ten minutes before we arrived, our cell rang; it was the host calling to say that the meeting had been cancelled because no one was coming. The next day, he promptly quit.
>
> Oh yes, and Scott's mother? She never did end up in the hospital.

In spite of the many challenges that they've faced, Amber and Dean continue to move forward, lean into the wind, and keep their eyes on their vision. Their favorite mantra is, "The more we expose, the more our check grows. What we lack in skill, we make up for in numbers." They remind me of what author, educator, and activist Parker L. Palmer wrote: "I will always have fears, but I need not be my fear, for I have other places within myself from which to speak and act."

Habit 6: Practicing Professional Perseverance

Perseverance is a by-product of all the other professional networking habits. One of the most frequent sayings in our profession is "Just don't quit!" Stories about the triumphs and struggles en route to financial freedom help sustain us. Of the many highly successful networkers I've met, Margie Aliprandi best exemplifies this sense of perseverance.

Today, Margie is an international speaker, author, and trainer; just 22 years ago she was a junior high music teacher. Within one year of starting her business, she was earning a five-figure monthly income; within three, she had achieved millionaire status.

Margie retired much later in her career and then reactivated two years later. She immediately set a goal to add 10 new Diamond Ambassadors (top leaders) to her team; she surpassed it when 24 Ambassadors walked across the stage to receive their awards at their next company convention. As a result, Margie was the first in her company to achieve the top rank of Crown Diamond. Her inspirational story exemplifies the habit of perseverance.

Margie had three strikes against her when she first started: no experience, no capital, and three small children (ages 2, 4, and 5). She had just renewed a teaching contract when she learned about a new networking company bringing an exciting product to market. Margie fell in love with the product. She had dreams of saving her home and providing a better life for her children, and realized her salary as a junior high music teacher just wouldn't cut it. She was at a crossroads in her life and, so, throwing caution to the wind, she cancelled her contract and started networking full-time. It wasn't easy, and Margie sacrificed a great deal during the first few years while kick-starting her business. She persisted, fumbling her way along in the face of doubts, fears, and high-stress activity. As she says, "I did it poorly until I did it well."

She often conducted three meetings a night, while family members babysat the children. Money was very tight, so when she led meetings in distant cities, she drove to them, parked in a hotel parking lot, slept in her car, and freshened up in a hotel washroom in the morning before walking into the meeting room, acting as if everything were "normal." When asked later how she felt about sleeping in her car during those tough days, she said she barely noticed; it was simply what she needed to do. Her *why*—her children's welfare—was so powerful that she pushed past any obstacles and focused on their future.

When I asked Margie how, as a single mom, she had managed her business, she replied, "Sometimes it was heartbreaking. I missed seeing my son's first home run in baseball because I was in a meeting. There were times when I wondered whether I was doing the right thing; I could still cry today over missing some of those key moments. It was ironic that I was building the business so that I could be with my children, yet it involved short-term pain for long-term happiness. But I would do it over again for the lifestyle we gained and the precious time we've had together."

Margie dealt with these hardships by getting her children on board early on in the process. She sat down with them and told them, "'I really need your support. I'm going to be away, but your grandma and grandpa will be with you.' They understood we were all in it together." But she also recalls:

One evening as I pulled out of the driveway on my way to yet another meeting, my son Todd came running out, in his soccer pajamas, crying. I pulled over and took him in my arms and felt his convulsing body against my chest and his tears on my cheek. I was crying, too. I was dead-tired, and the last thing I wanted was to leave him. But I said, "Sweetie, please go into the house. Be a big boy and I promise you that one day I will take you with me everywhere I go."

Margie kept her promise. Today, her four children are grown and they have experienced the world together with their mother; and their idea of family has expanded to include people from all over the globe. Her children also have had the privilege of watching their mother mentor people internationally. While still actively building her networking business, she says,

My greatest role today is cheerleading people for their large and small successes, loving them, and helping them feel "seen" for who they are and the greatness they possess. My children's lives are richer for the experiences, and for what they've witnessed in a mom who persevered through self-doubt. When I look at them now, I see the people that they have become due in part to my entrepreneurial example. Perhaps I was a better mom because I was living my dream—and in the process enabled them to believe in the ability to achieve their dreams.

As mentioned previously, early on Margie conducted countless meetings. One day she flew to a meeting in New York. Upon arrival at the airport, she grabbed a cab, but the taxi driver got lost and she arrived quite late. She was greeted by a small number of guests who weren't exactly excited about being there and were disgruntled by Margie's lateness. The fact that only a small number showed up didn't faze her, though, because she had long ago given up expecting the number that the host had confirmed. To her, it was just par for the course.

Margie got through the meeting and was relieved when it was over. As she was gathering her presentation materials, a Russian man approached her and said, in a thick accent, "I will take this to

Russia." She calmly nodded and replied, "Okay; good." She didn't allow herself to get too excited, though; she'd heard plenty of promises before.

She flew back home and thought nothing more about the Russian's promise—until a few months later when she began to notice a few Russian names on her organizational sales summary. Within a short time, her organization included about 500,000 Russian distributors. The stack of printout paper with Russian names was 8 to 10 inches deep. And that was just the beginning of what became a huge international organization that encompassed Eurasia, South Asia and beyond.

PERSEVERE THROUGH PLANTING SEEDS EVERY DAY

It's helpful to remember that there is a sowing season and a reaping season, and they don't occur at the same time. Sometimes, it seems to take forever to reap the harvest; but, as Margie Aliprandi says, "Keep sowing seeds, persevere, and don't expect all to grow, because the sun will scorch some of them. You cannot sow two seeds and expect a big harvest. The 80/20 rule is alive and well here, so plant seeds every day if you want your business to thrive."

Once you go through the process of achievement, you will be able to replicate its success principles anytime, because perseverance will have become a habit. Until then, use the following affirmation to help assimilate perseverance: *I persevere and bounce back easily from temporary setbacks.* Also, make it a habit to use mental imagery to see yourself building your business with confidence and courage.

Chapter 10

PRACTICAL WAYS TO GROW A HIGHLY PROFITABLE BUSINESS

Valerie Bates

Success is achieved by accepting sole responsibility for your entire business—including the company and team with which you align yourself. It also requires that you mentor yourself, adopt the right attitude and perspectives, and develop professional habits. Upon that foundation, master five major competencies and over time you've got it made in terms of developing a highly profitable business.

Rest assured that learning each of the five skill sets is not complicated. It does not take a lot of studying, but it does involve a healthy attitude toward learning. By that I mean it's not unlike learning to ride a bike where you perfect your skills by falling down a few times, brushing yourself off, and getting back up for ongoing attempts. Practice really does make perfect, especially when you have a credible team leader coaching you along the way.

FIVE MAJOR COMPETENCIES

The five major competencies in building a highly profitable networking business, include the ability to:

1. Build a tremendous network
2. Expose/Invite people to take a look at your products and business
3. Present the whole story about your business
4. Follow-up and validate the information
5. Support and lead your team.

COMPETENCY 1: HOW TO BUILD A TREMENDOUS NETWORK

Your contact list is your greatest asset. Build it in your mind first by envisioning a huge network and filling in the blank spaces with names later on. Think locally, nationally and internationally. Make it expansive and understand that it takes time, endless seed planting and reaching out in order to eventually realize a tremendous network.

Although we're primarily interested here in the benefits of a large network for your networking business, the value of building one extends far beyond developing a group of people to whom you can offer a business opportunity and products. The rate of change and degree of uncertainty we experience today makes the strength and reach of a personal network increasingly important. Think of the process of building a network as "positive" networking where you're connecting with individuals you like, trust, and can interact with throughout your lifetime. You always want to look at the broader perspective and think long term when building your network; and keep in mind how crucial it is not to alienate anyone—*ever*!

The first rule of building a network is to treat all contacts like gold, whether they're close friends, acquaintances, or "cold" connections. And always remember that "weak" contacts, even distant acquaintances, often can be more powerful forces in your network than close friends. Research has proven the strength of these weak ties in social networks. Sociologist Mark Granovetter, in a landmark study, looked at several hundred professional and technical workers in the United States. It showed that half learned about their positions through personal contacts, and only 16 percent of those saw their contact "often." More than 55 percent saw that contact only "occasionally." These statistics demonstrate that even those individuals with whom you interact only sporadically represent far more social power than that of your close friends. Your personal network is connected to other networks that are both strong and weak. You never know when a contact has his or her own contact that is looking for a solution to his or her financial problems, and your business may be the answer to that second contact's prayers.

There are countless ways to build your network, but the best is to simply implement a few tried-and-true strategies that capitalize on your strengths. Once you've mastered those, then by all means add more to your repertoire. People will often dabble in countless methods when building a network, but fail to develop any of them fully and effectively because their approach is too scattered.

Secrets to Growing a Network

Again, your contact list is your greatest asset. You don't need to invest a lot of money in developing that asset, but you do need to put forth time and effort, and be consistent. Make sure to add new contacts every day, to keep your list dynamic and constantly growing. When you fail to add contacts regularly, you will eventually run out of assets — the equivalent of going bankrupt in a traditional business.

Secret 1: Start with Your Top 25 List
First, make a "warm market" list of 25 people you know. Brainstorm names without making judgments, and record those that come to mind in a notebook or on your contact management system. If it makes it easier, think of this as your "wedding" or "birthday" list.

Second, make a note beside the names of potential business partners according to the following criteria:

1. They are optimistic. (Pessimists rarely, if ever, succeed in networking.)

2. They have credibility and influence in their communities.
3. They are coachable. (In other words, open to learning.)
4. You would enjoy working with them because . . .

Start by contacting those who live in your area so that it's easier to bond with them and form a team that fosters energy, loyalty, and a sense of community. Of course, it's also important to contact those farther away, but it's preferable to start in your own "backyard" and branch out from there.

Third, make a note of those who are potential retail customers. Ask yourself, "Who are people I don't want to do business with but who would benefit from the products my company sells?" They will, potentially, become your first retail customers.

You will be paid on how well you move products through your distribution channel comprised of retail customers as well as business builders who use your products. Although most of the discussion in this book focuses on recruiting business partners, retailing is essential to developing a profitable business. You must, therefore, continuously acquire customers, both through directly promoting products to retail customers and through those who may have studied your business and declined to participate as business partners, but want to use your products as customers.

Fourth, work with an upline team member who is supportive, fully engaged in the business, and knowledgeable about exposing people to the opportunity. Practice your inviting skills with that partner until you are comfortable executing them. Then make your calls.

If there is someone on your list who would be helpful in honing your skills ask that person to allow you to practice with him or her, too. You can determine this by asking yourself, "Who in my life is most supportive and will provide sincere, helpful, and honest feedback?" Then call on that person for assistance.

Secret 2: Every Sparrow Knows an Eagle and Every Minnow Knows a Whale

A very effective way to grow your network is to ask for referrals from every person who listens to your presentation and declines to join you. You can expand it substantially by tapping into these "lukewarm" leads. The problem is that most new networkers don't bother to ask for support from those who are often willing to assist.

Let's assume that you're an independent business owner with a health and wellness company, and you've just finished a presentation to your friend Cherie, who indicates that she's not interested right now. Before you part ways, you ask, "Cherie, will you do me a big favor and help me develop more connections? I want to expand my network. Whom would you contact if you were in my shoes? Who do you know that is into health, and is also somewhat entrepreneurial? Who is your favorite chiropractor? How about your favorite fitness instructor or coach?" Also ask Cherie how she knows these individuals, and request permission to use her name when you contact them. Doing so will allow you to turn a cold lead into a lukewarm one—as long as Cherie is credible. Remember the power of these so-called weak links; they can actually turn out to be fairly strong leads.

Secret 3: Use Social Networking

Social networking blends technology and social interaction and plays a significant role in communication today. Some networkers use this platform to reinforce their teams and keep them informed; they share photos, publicly edify team members, recognize achievements, and share inspirational quotes and video clips. All of this has a positive effect on team culture.

Without a doubt, social media is a great way to connect with like-minded people with whom you have something in common. You can update them about what's going on in your life and share information that you feel will be of value to them. Be sure to build a relationship first, and then list your business site on your profile so that viewers can choose whether to click through to another site and learn more about you, your products, and business. This contrasts to the approach that people take when they introduce themselves to someone on a social networking site and promote a business or products immediately. A lot of people use social media as a channel through which to bombard others with advertisements; they fail to realize that social networking is truly about relationships *first*. Most people nowadays are experiencing information overload, and will not respond favorably to spam or advertisements.

One new networker on my team posted the following message to her 200-plus friends on Facebook, against my advice: "Hey! I just started a new business and I need some business partners. Interested?" She tipped her hat to every single online connection and was disheartened when not one person responded. This is the equivalent of walking into a party and yelling the same thing. People do not want to be "sold" on anything.

Social networking also is excellent for reconnecting with people from your past: school friends, college classmates, neighbors, colleagues, service providers, and relatives. If you want to talk business, send them a personal message first and arrange to connect over the phone. Online, you can say something like, "Hi, Cindy! It's been too long! What's the best number to reach you now? Want to catch up." When you connect over the phone, listen carefully to what Cindy has to say, and then—and only if it seems appropriate—talk about your products and business. Start the business conversation by telling her you've launched a business and thought of her because [sincere compliment]. You must use your social skills wisely and show genuine concern for what is best for others. Proceed on that basis, and you can't go wrong.

Regardless of how talented and adept you may be at connecting via social media and gaining free publicity through free e-zines, blogs, Facebook, Twitter, YouTube, or LinkedIn, you will ultimately want to take your efforts offline and interact with people in "real life." To that end, you can invite them to live events like business conference calls and webinars.

By all means, use social media as *one* means of building daily connections. Block out the time you'll spend to do so, however, so that you don't allow it to supersede the need to grow your network in other ways as well, many of which are discussed in this book.

Secret 4: Build through Local Events

Duplication is the key to building a network, and one of the best ways to do that is through small, duplicable local meetings. Though the popularity of technology has put in-person meetings out of favor with many these days, many of today's fastest-growing companies are using the local meeting approach effectively. They are using both meetings and technology, of course; but generally, people value the energy, trust, and sense of community that face-to-face teamwork generates.

You always want to begin by taking baby steps. Start with small meetings of four to six people, in your home; then, when your team grows, your leaders can duplicate and hold meetings in *their* homes. Once you have a sufficient number of in-home meetings taking place in your city, you can sponsor a larger meeting with your entire organization every few months while continuing to hold the smaller meetings.

People like teams that look like they're "going somewhere" and will often join based on seeing numbers of others moving forward in the business. They want social proof, so to speak, and when they see that you are serious about building, and watch as a growing number of people come on board, they will be more likely to enroll in the program, too.

Business growth snowballs locally over time, through reliable effort and good leadership. The secret is to hold consistent, interesting, and positive meetings that build spirit and cooperation.

Secret 5: Use a Triggering Device

It's amazing how an effective triggering device can remind us of individuals in our distant networks. Such a device can jump-start your memory and help you recall names you otherwise wouldn't be able to pull out of the black hole of your subconscious. Good "memory joggers" will help you remember at least 200 more people beyond those on your Top 25 List. Online career lists or Yellow Pages will remind you of professionals you've bought services from over the years, such as: your banker, tailor, hair stylist, shop owner, fitness instructor, massage therapist, teacher, web designer, professor, plumber, contractor, dog groomer, coach, doctor, lawyer, teacher, insurance broker, financial advisor, baker, housecleaner, or day care provider. One name will trigger even more names, and your list will grow exponentially as your brain begins to make connections.

Secret 6: Include Potential Retail Customers on Your List

Get in the habit each day of adding potential retail customer names to your network. Use a trigger list to help you come up with associations and individuals in various service industries that would be a natural fit for your products.

One of the best ways to earn a check quickly is to retail your products. Though this book focuses primarily on how to recruit business partners, let's remember that we all want customers. Some independent business owners utilize the Internet to do their retailing, and this can be very effective for those who have that skill set, or are willing to invest in developing it. I know of one particular team whose members shared the cost of designing an effective product website; they invested in getting it to appear at the top of search engine result lists, and have established a strong retail customer base. They are committed to making it work, and their product line is conducive to online sales.

The Internet option for retail sales is open to each of us. Just be sure to investigate thoroughly before you decide to go that direction, as this approach isn't for everyone; it requires the investment of significant time and money to make it work. One of the first thoughts some new distributors have is that they'll market their products online. They assume that having a website makes it a viable option. But this isn't something in which you can just dabble. It takes knowledge, effort, and financial investment to make it work.

Every new distributor will want to acquire at least 10 retail customers immediately, continue growing their customer base, and following up. Naturally, the degree of emphasis you place on retailing will depend on your personal interests, compensation plan, products, and, of course, desire to earn immediate cash. Most networkers today use online ordering, and sign retail customers onto autoship, an automated monthly order. Customers tend to be very loyal to the consumable products they love and use consistently. Personally, I've been using the same products from one network marketing company for over 30 years.

Secret 7: Understand the "Needs and Wants" Mystery

Don't be disappointed if someone you have added to your network list, and that you think should be open to your business opportunity or products, isn't. Remember the issue of timing, and keep in mind the four-room apartment model: contentment, denial, confusion, and renewal. It can be applied to potential retail customers as well as business partners.

Although certain individuals may look like they *need* your products, they won't necessarily *want* them. We can all relate to this; for example, although we *need* to get in shape, we may not *want* to get up at six in the morning to jog or lift weights. So even though it's clear that Uncle Harry needs to lose 30 pounds, it doesn't automatically follow that he'll want to buy your weight-loss product, no matter how great it is. He may not be ready to start a weight-loss program right now. Don't take people's negative responses personally, and don't prejudge them. Just put their names down on your list, contact them, and go with the flow.

Secret 8: Develop a Global List

Many networking companies are "going global" these days. If that describes your company, you'll want to add international connections to your contact list. One way to expand globally without leaving home is to network with local people who have connections in another country. Encourage them to network locally in their communities, and find those with the best connections elsewhere. Do you recall from Chapter 9 Margie Aliprandi's experience with the Russian man? By sponsoring a person in your country who knows someone in another country, you can potentially develop an international business without ever leaving home.

Secret 9: Maintain a Full Network to Improve Your Professional Posture

When you keep growing your list, you are less apt to pressure people into doing things they don't want to do—whether it's to join your company or buy your products. As Mark says, "A person agreeing against his or her will is of the same opinion still." Having other people in the pipeline at all times will help you get past rejection quickly and prevent you from fixating on a single candidate. It will also help you develop a confident posture, which will communicate to others that you are moving forward with or without them. Instead of feeling discouraged when someone declines, you'll look forward to getting in touch with the next contact on your list.

COMPETENCY 2: HOW TO EXPOSE/INVITE

You might expect that inviting would come naturally to most of us, since we've been asking people to dinner and birthday parties, concerts, coffee, holiday celebrations, sporting events, and more, for years . We've been "inviting" for so long that we often do so without giving it a second thought. We simply call or e-mail and ask people to join us somewhere, for some event. No problem, right?

But once we enter network marketing and want to invite local people to check out our business over a cup of coffee, at lunch, a private business reception (PBR), business launch party, meeting, tasting party, makeup party, fitness information session, or skin care clinic, and we stumble all over ourselves. Why? Because we've added a new component that changes it from a habitual to conscious act. Just the thought of inviting people to do anything in this context renders many nervous and tongue-tied. They may lose any sense of individuality and robotically read from a script. Their confidence wanes; they sound hesitant—and then wonder why individuals decline to even take a look.

Here's how to overcome the obstacles many of us face when we're introducing or inviting people to take a look at our business:

First, decide before you ever pick up the phone that you will *not* give them too much information; if you do, they may conclude that they've got enough to make a decision, even though they don't have the whole story. This approach is neither fair to them nor productive for you. The better approach is to say something like, "I only have a few minutes now; I'm just getting started in this and can't do it justice over the phone. Come over on Tuesday and I'll fill you in on all the details." Or, if you're calling long distance, you might say, "I only have a few minutes, and I'm just getting started, so would you please check out this website? It'll do a lot better job of explaining it than I can at this point. Grab a pen and I'll give you the information you'll need to check it out." Otherwise, you'll spill the beans and ruin their research. Make a promise to yourself beforehand that you will keep your calls short and on track.

Second, ask yourself several questions before you pick up the phone: Where are these people hurting in their lives? What are their wants or dreams? What are their hot buttons? How might your business help them solve their problems or enhance their situation? What is the history of your relationship with them? Why have you decided to call them? What special qualities do they have that you admire? What is your goal in calling them? Your answers to these questions will help you make the calls more meaningful and specific to each of them.

Third, *practice*. Ask someone you consider the most supportive person in your world to help you rehearse and give you feedback. Call your best upline leader and practice with him or her. The more you rehearse this conversation, the easier it will become; in no time, inviting people to check out your business will become as naturally to you as if you were inviting them to a party.

Fourth, be very clear on your goal when speaking with these individuals. Your goal is to get them to agree to check out whatever exposure tool your team is using, or to meet with you for 30 to 60 minutes. After a brief personal chat, tell them that you are calling because you've started a new business and you thought of them right away because . . . At this point, pay them a sincere compliment that pertains to why you did think of them. Tell them that you are excited about your company, love the products, and are calling to invite them to . . . (check out a website or sizzle call — any exposure tool you prefer — or a meeting). Emphasize that you're simply asking them to check it out. Tell them that if they want more information afterward, you will provide it for them, but that you'll also respect their decision if they aren't interested. Mention that you only want to work with those people who are a good match. This statement takes the pressure off everyone. Finally, if they agree to check out the information, or meet with you, arrange a mutually convenient date and time to connect.

If you've invited people who live elsewhere to check out an exposure tool, call them back and ask them what they liked about the tool. Then take them to the next step by directing them to a website that offers a full presentation or business story. But before we discuss the skill set you'll need for a presentation, let's first cover a few more important aspects of the exposure, or invitation, part of the process.

Secrets for Effective Exposure/Inviting Skills

Recently, a relatively new business partner, Juan, called with a problem I'd heard many times before: "I'm talking to a whole lot of people and getting nowhere," he complained, "and I can't figure out where I'm going wrong. Can you help me pinpoint exactly what my problem is?"

I coached him on the following proven techniques to increase the power of his exposures, after which he was able to guide more prospects into a full presentation. The following are 10 secrets that will work for you, too:

1. Remember that exposure is all about *sorting*, not *convincing*. You're looking for people who are looking for you; they're open to business options.
2. Limit all initial contacts to three *postured* minutes, maximum in which you maintain your confidence.
3. Create sufficient intrigue to inspire people to spend a few minutes in initial research.
4. Remember the four "W's" slogan: "Some will, some won't; so what, someone's waiting!"
5. Realize that a prospect's response to an exposure tool rests mainly on whether or not the timing is right in his or her life.
6. If your prospect is new to networking, do not conduct a full presentation until you've shown him or her an intriguing short piece of information, like an exposure call.

7. Get the person to check out your business specifically after the exposure step. Lead with the *opportunity first and product second.* This way, your prospect may consider becoming a retail customer even if he or she doesn't go for the business. Be aware, however, if you start with the product and the person turns it down, there's no way he or she can agree to build a business built on a product he or she doesn't appreciate.
8. Pick a daily exposure number, between 5 or 10 and 30 contacts, and commit to it. Why not select it now? What is it?
9. Remember that rich networkers keep the exposure step simple and doable, and they do it *much* more frequently than poor networkers.
10. Let tools do the talking for you. A tool might be a sample product, a short sizzle call, CD, DVD, brochure, website, opportunity call, or webinar.

COMPETENCY 3: HOW TO PRESENT THE WHOLE STORY

Presenting the whole story involves painting a complete picture of the trends to which your company is responding (i.e., positioning); the special team with which you're working; the company's credibility, products, and compensation; and how the business and products can help them achieve their dreams.

Secrets to Effective Presentations

Again, the tools will do the talking for you, so your primary role is to move the due diligence process along and ensure that you're responding to the candidates' needs. The following secrets will help you do that effectively. Remember your role as "director of due diligence."

Secret 1: Tailor Presentations to Your Candidates' Needs
Before you walk candidates through your favorite presentation tool, ask questions to uncover more about *their needs.* After telling your own story about how you got started (two to three minutes, max), a good way to proceed is to ask, for example, "Katrina, if you could

wave a magic wand and change one thing that would have a significant impact on your life, what would that be?" Katrina's answer will provide insight into her aspirations and allow you to show her that your business may be the solution she needs. You can always ask a different question; just make sure it's one that effectively opens up a discussion about aspirations.

Secret 2: Build Your Personal Credibility

Prospects are more likely to talk about themselves if you share your own story about why you started your business (again, no longer than two or three minutes). The way you tell the story is important—not just the words you use, but also the authenticity you express as you tell it. The key is, simply, to be *you*; people will appreciate sincerity when you tell them how and why you got started, what's happened since then, and where you're planning to go. Your enthusiasm also will attract people, since most respond to positive energy and connect with personal stories more so than with facts and numbers. Remember the saying: "Facts tell; stories sell." Your personal story is, therefore, incredibly important.

Secret 3: Build Company Credibility

Whichever presentation tool you use should establish credibility for the company, owners, products, compensation plan, and trends that are in your favor. As in the exposure step, let the tools do the talking in your presentation, but be sure to add a personal touch, to establish trust and credibility. Presentation tools might include a website, company presentation booklet (hard copy or digital), or corporate DVD. Show candidates only one to begin with, as it can be overwhelming to hit them with a firehose worth of information, even in the presentation. A slower drip of material is more effective, since most people have fairly short attention spans.

If you're sending candidates to a complex website, tell them exactly where they can find the most important items, such as the compensation plan and product listing. If they can get online as you're talking, walk through parts of the site with them, hitting the highlights. They can study the whole thing later on, on their own. Right now, you want to get to know them better, and give them the basics benefits of on the company, products, and compensation plan.

Secret 4: Build Product Credibility and Enthusiasm

Your entire presentation is centered on two issues: the *business opportunity* and the *tangible products and/or services* and what they can do for the candidate. The quality of the products will drive your entire business. Without worthwhile offerings that people love and will continue to use day after day for years to come, your business will falter. You cannot build a distribution channel on hot air or second-rate goods. You must be distributing highly effective, fairly priced products; our business depends on word-of-mouth marketing through relationships.

Every company needs at least one "sizzle" product—an item that people will love so much that they'll talk about it to their friends and family, and drive sales volume. It must be unique, patented, and proprietary—which means that people cannot find it on store shelves. You will go out of business if your product is available through retail outlets. A good company must protect you from that situation.

There is nothing more important than your belief in the products. Without the ability to offer something that the masses demand, your business simply will not fly. Most people tend to overstudy product ingredients and formulation processes, rather than using them and developing their own testimonials about *results*. Once you become your own best customer, you will sell a lot more product—and convince a lot more people to do the same.

Secret 5: Show How They Can Earn Money—Fast Cash and Long-Term Income

It's important that your tool simplifies the compensation plan discussion. Think about what candidates really need—and want—to know, which is: "How do I earn money? How much can I earn, and how fast?" They'll also want to hear about residual income and the long-term potential. Stick with addressing those issues; don't bore them with a detailed walkthrough of your plan. They can review it in detail later and call you if they have questions.

Keep in mind that stories work in all aspects of your presentation, including those about earning capacity. Keep this one real, too; do not build up false expectations regarding the speed with which candidates can earn big money. We all know that a legitimate business requires hard work, skill development, and perseverance. Legitimate network marketing companies are not right for people who want fast, easy money; they should seek their fortunes elsewhere.

Secret 6: Continue Moving the Process Forward

Upon completing your presentation, ask candidates what questions they have. Answer these questions as best you can, and indicate that you would like to introduce a team leader you respect to give them another perspective, as well. If you've covered a fair amount of ground and the timing seems right, feel free to say at some point during your discussion, "I think it would be a good idea for you to talk to my partner, who's been at this longer than I have. If you've got a few minutes now, I'll get her on the phone." Then describe why you respect that person. You want to let your potential business partners know that they will be part of an amazing team if they join your endeavor.

Do not leave this presentation step without confirming the commitment of the candidates regarding the next step—whether it's meeting your team leader, visiting additional websites, listening to a live opportunity call, or accompanying you to a meeting. At this point, you're moving into the third critical skill set in networking: following up or validating.

COMPETENCY 4: HOW TO FOLLOW-UP AND VALIDATE

People generally accept that establishing trust takes several interactions and meetings; it doesn't happen overnight. *Validation* is the process by which you provide further proof of the validity of the business, products, and your team, along with evidence that this is a promising venture for them—*if* they're willing to work hard and learn the right skills. The entire process is designed to increase the candidates' excitement about what they are learning.

Secrets to Effective Follow-up or Validation

Some people neglect to follow up with candidates because they are not disciplined enough to schedule callbacks, either at the end of their last meeting or within 24 hours of the initial contact. But prospects are often scattered in their focus, as well, and it is up to us as independent business owners to help them stay on track and complete their research. When you don't follow up promptly, they assume that you are not serious about your business. It's vital to keep the following phrase in mind during this phase: "The fortune is in the follow-up."

Secret 1: Provide Further Proof

Validation involves providing further "proof," and this requires tuning in carefully to candidates' needs. This might involve simply directing them to a different website, a brochure, CD, DVD, testimonials, growth charts, opportunity calls, or publications; or it might require giving them samples of the products. Typically, it takes several contacts, discussions, and sources of information before prospects have what they need to make an informed decision.

Secret 2: Arrange a Validation Call with a Respected Leader

One of the most important tools you can use is a validation call with your respected team leader, as he or she will provide further credibility. Candidates are attracted to a strong team when they realize that a top-quality leader will be available to help with their validation calls should they decide to build a business. Through this contact they will understand that they will be in business *for* themselves but not *by* themselves.

One common mistake network marketers make during this phase is to try to go it alone rather than involve a competent team member in the validation process. This is necessary at any point in your career in network marketing, regardless of how long you've been in the business.

Discuss with your leader whether you should be present on these validation calls. Some leaders prefer that you not be and will ask you to leave a message and they will call your prospect back themselves. This can be unfortunate because being privy to these calls is excellent training. You need to work out the process to satisfy both of you. If you will participate on the calls, refrain from speaking too much. Introduce your leader and jump in only when he or she asks you to do so. Your role is to make the introduction and then listen and learn. Once you've participated in about 15 or more of these calls, you will be ready to conduct your own validations for your team. However, you will continue to call on your upline leader for third-party validation for your personal prospects.

Secret 3: Ask the Right Questions to Move Candidates toward a Decision

Another important element of the validation process is asking questions. There are times when it's a good idea to "test the water," to see where the candidate is in terms of making a decision. How do you handle that? Pick one of the following questions based on your relationship with the person to help you learn what he or she needs:

- What would you like to do next?
- What else do you need to help you make a decision?
- How close are you right now to getting started, on a scale of 1 to 10?
- What would it take to move you to a 10?
- What do you think?
- How are you feeling about this right now? Isn't it exciting?!
- Where do you see yourself fitting in?
- Are you ready to get started?

COMPETENCY 5: HOW TO SUPPORT AND LEAD YOUR TEAM

Leadership is absolutely crucial to supporting your team, and you will learn more in the next two chapters, which are dedicated to that subject. (Note: The length at which leadership is covered in this book indicates the degree of value and importance it has in network marketing.) Leading volunteers is very different from leading within a hierarchical structure.

Secrets to Effective Support

Secret 1: Help New Team Members Get Started Immediately

Your role as a leader in helping team members get started immediately and correctly is critical. You also will serve as their coach as they begin to develop skills in exposing/inviting, presenting, and validating. (Your respected upline team member will handle this for you until you are competent yourself. And most companies also have training programs to aid in this effort.)

The importance of reliable support cannot be overstated; the majority of new business owners who are left to sink or swim generally sink. Your goal is twofold: to teach them "to swim" and to serve as an early check to help them build faith and resilience.

Secret 2: Conduct a Strategy Session

New leaders should ask their team leader to participate with them in a strategy session with any new partners, to help these newcomers do the following:

- Access company or team leader training.
- Find the most important resources and be apprised when calls are scheduled.
- Meet your best upline leaders (provide their phone numbers and other contact information).
- Clarify their "why," vision, and goals one to three years out. (Ask: "Where do you see yourself one year from now?" What's driving you to do this business? — if you don't already know.)
- Determine whether their expectations are realistic, relative to their time commitment and skill level.
- Help them to write their Top 25 List, and discuss who they put on it, and why.
- Practice the inviting process. (Set up sessions to do so with you or your upline team.)
- Enlist their first two or more business partners, and then help them do the same for these partners.

- Use the resources in this book.
- Complete a 90-day launch and relaunch, just as you are doing (see the next section).

Secret 3: Teach Them a "Due Diligence" Perspective

Finally, when coaching your team, to help reduce their anxiety and improve the chances of their achieving positive long-term results, encourage them to take this approach: "I'm not here to determine if this business is right for you. It's certainly worthwhile investigating. It may or may not be a good fit, but you'll never know until you conduct your own due diligence."

A 90-DAY GAME PLAN TO LAUNCH AND RELAUNCH YOUR BUSINESS

The objective of a 90-day game plan is to block out, roughly, a three-month time frame during which you'll concentrate on launching or relaunching your business. Keep in mind Sisyphus repeatedly rolling the boulder up a hill, and the level of concentrated effort it takes to overcome inertia and get the ball rolling down the other side. The same principle is at work with the 90-day game plan. It takes tremendous effort to kick-start your business, but once you're on a roll, the momentum accelerates, and you can just keep going.

People tend to respond well to 90-day spurts of concentrated focus, whether it's a plan to lose weight or build a business. For most, three months is enough time to adopt the professional habits required to build a network, recruit business partners and customers, and support a team. Once these skills become habitual, you will be able to launch and sustain a viable business.

How to Launch and Relaunch Your Business

Follow this 10-step process to help launch your business with focus and consistency every 90 days. Use this same process with your team.

1. Write down a detailed description of what your business will look like 90 days from your launch/relaunch date.

2. Break down that description into how it will look in 60 and then 30 days from the launch date. Include the following:
   - How much money you're earning
   - The number of business partners you have
   - The size of your team
   - Your advancement level; key partners' levels
   - The number of partners and team members accompanying you to the next meeting or convention

3. Choose a partner you respect, someone who is also launching or relaunching his or her business on a 90-day plan. Keep each other accountable.

4. Share your goals with your partner or a supportive person. Verbalizing them will help you commit to them.

5. Break down each of your goals into specific activities, to help you reach them more easily. Focus on the number of exposures/invitations you will make daily. Once you have made enough exposures/invitations, you will be able to document the number of presentations, validations, new customers, and business partners using the worksheet at the end of this chapter.

6. Schedule daily time blocks for business building on your calendar.

7. Use the Accountability Worksheet provided in Table 10.1 to track your progress. Feedback keeps you on track.

8. Listen, watch, and/or read something inspirational each day to keep your momentum going.

9. Celebrate your successes, goal by goal. Recognize your partner's achievements as well.

10. As a leader, demonstrate for your team how to launch and relaunch their business every 90 days.

It takes at least 90 days to firmly establish the habits that are critical for building a highly profitable business. Once you have successfully done so, you will have the skills, perspectives, and attitude necessary to fully realize financial independence and the rich life you've dreamed of.

Table 10.1   Launch and Relaunch Accountability Worksheet

Day	Number of Invitations/ Exposures	Number of Presentations	Number of Validations	Number of New Customers	Number of New Partners
1.					
2.					
3.					
4.					
5.					
6.					
7.					
8.					
9.					
10.					
11.					
12.					
13.					
14.					
15.					
16.					
17.					
18.					
19.					
20.					
21.					
22.					
23.					
24.					
25.					
26.					
27.					
28.					
29.					
30.					
31.					

Chapter 11

HOW TO RECOGNIZE PEOPLE AND CIRCUMSTANCES THAT CAN POISON YOUR POTENTIAL

Mark Yarnell

It's amazing how many toxic people there are in the world—both those who never mean to cause us harm and those who seem to delight in it. There are also toxic actions, some from which many of us can never seem to recover. Many great men and women have entered our profession and quit immediately after encountering what I am about to describe in this chapter, which is a tool for helping you anticipate and avoid or deal with such challenges.

Consider the following metaphor; it is an appropriate one here. I call it the Toxic Bomb Field, and I introduced it in Valerie and my previous work, *The Holy Grail of Network Marketing*.

Imagine that you and I, along with 20 others, are standing on the outer edge of a beautiful field. Green, six-inch-high wheat is blowing in a gentle breeze as far as the eye can see. It's sunny, 72 degrees, and a breathtaking rainbow arches in the distance. We have a tour guide who is responsible for assisting us on a one-mile walk through this field. On the other side, at the bottom of the glorious rainbow, is the proverbial pot of gold—with your name on it.

Our guide hands each of us a pair of binoculars and suggests that we view the rainbow more closely through them. We discover that he is indeed telling the truth about the pot of gold. In fact, there are several pots, each containing $28 million. We also see a large group of well-dressed people who have already made the trek; and a number of expensive cars belonging to them are parked in a small lot nearby. Each person on the other side of the rainbow is smiling or waving; and several are holding up signs that say, "You can do it, too! Come join us!"

The tour guide gives us simple instructions: to cross the field as slowly or rapidly as we wish, and then claim our $28 million upon our arrival. The field is one square mile. Initially, all of us stand around looking at each other in utter disbelief, until eventually one person takes off running, followed by several others.

Suddenly, there are two small explosions. Those of us who haven't started across the field notice body parts airborne in a cloud of thick smoke. As we look on in horror, our guide says, "Oh, I neglected to mention that there are quite a few land mines buried in the field. It's possible that some of you may become amputees by making the trip. You may have noticed that some of the people on the other side are missing arms, legs, or feet. But I can promise you that nobody has died so far—and some got through without stepping on a mine! And those who lost a limb or two claim that their $28 million prize was well worth it. So it's off to the races!"

How would you react? Probably, most in the group would immediately walk away in shock, while others would stand reflectively and consider the odds. No doubt a few really bright ones would spend the time necessary to learn how to anticipate, recognize, and diffuse the land mines before ever setting out. And those who chose to go across would make certain that the guide was a land mine expert who still had all his limbs. Most of us probably wouldn't roll the dice and follow a person who had just "gotten lucky" and made it to the other side safely, limbs intact, regardless of how much we believed we too could blunder onto the same path he had taken.

Welcome to the wonderful world of network marketing. While I've never met anyone who's lost a limb in our field, I have encountered more than a few poor souls who have lost their self-esteem, families, and friends—*and* seen their dreams and goals blown to smithereens. Some were highly educated doctors and lawyers, while others were successful executives or well-known celebrity athletes. Some had been very skilled, straight-commissioned salespeople, whereas others had been owners of huge, successful companies. Most were just decent, hard-working men and women trying to better themselves. Many were much more talented than most and had every skill necessary to succeed.

But they failed, for one simple reason: Nobody warned them about the toxic land mines they'd encounter along the way, or gave them a survival guide. So they set out without the ability to anticipate, recognize, and overcome the obstacles they would inevitably face on their network marketing journey.

I have, therefore, written this chapter to teach you how to do exactly that: anticipate, recognize, and diffuse those bombs. And make no mistake: This field is laden with mines. Just because you don't see them doesn't mean they aren't there.

This isn't meant to scare you off or intimidate you. Though the mines are all around you, they are easy to deal with once you know exactly what they look like and how to anticipate them.

Consider the following: Millions of people will play 18 holes of golf this week. Many will show up with the best equipment money can buy. They will never attempt to join the PGA or go on tour, and no one will criticize them for having no desire to turn pro. Network marketing is very similar to this. A few people make the necessary sacrifices to earn the big bucks, but most are content to just enjoy the game. Those who do make it to the top of either profession must develop skills that the masses will never attempt to perfect.

This chapter focuses on two unavoidable and well-documented facts. First, as just outlined, there are land mines everywhere in this industry, in the form of both toxic people and circumstances. Second, those land mines are set to detonate at different times, based on the particular steps being taken. That means anyone, regardless of experience, can step on one of these bombs at any time. That is why both new recruits and seasoned veterans must learn to anticipate and diffuse each one, regardless of when or where it appears.

Among the numerous winners I've interviewed over the years, there is pretty much universal acceptance that there are five steps that must be taken to build a strong network marketing organization. Independent of the company or products, pay plan, or management team, networkers must accomplish five tasks: They must expose, present, validate, enroll, and support in order to succeed.

The reason no one is safe from land mines is that they surface during each of the five different steps. The further we progress in the recruiting process, the more likely we are to miss the more well-camouflaged bombs—that's just human nature. We tend to ignore those potential bombs—which may appear because we want to protect our investment—once we've invested more and more time with a given prospect.

Scientists call this tendency *loss aversion* and it's the same human characteristic that allows rational investors to hang onto stocks well after they've tanked; they hate to lose their principle. Some convince themselves that the company they've invested in will make a comeback, even after the owners are in jail. As such, the more time seasoned veterans invest in new business associates, the more difficult it is to cut their losses and move on. However, if you want to make the big money, you must have the will to walk away from toxic people and circumstances, as quickly as possible.

MAPPING THE TOXIC BOMBS

My hope is that by mapping these land mines and providing survival strategies will motivate you to avoid them and move forward. Because many of the land mines are harder to spot as you move through the five-step process, those that people encounter most frequently are often not discovered until they reach the support stage. That's where the mines can really blow up and do the most damage, even to veterans in the field. My goal here is to save you as best I can from the toxic shocks.

Toxic Bomb 1: The Irrelevant Minutiae Accessory

People are cognitively hardwired, just like other animals. We love rewards, and we repeat behaviors especially when they result in rewards. Scientifically speaking, when we experience the pleasure brought on by a dopamine surge in our brains, we seek that same reward by repeating the behavior that triggered it. Most addiction specialists learned years ago that individuals with healthy self-control can walk away from mood-altering substances like alcohol and cocaine; sadly, many can't. And therein lies the danger.

Drugs and alcohol seem like great "therapy" until the people using them lose control of their intake, which often happens when they need more of whatever it is they're using to experience the same high. The substance of addiction that's most detrimental to today's professionals isn't a particular drug or drink, however; it's cell phones. These are wonderful communication tools, until people lose the ability to use them wisely. The problem is simple: When some kind of noise—a bell or vibration, for instance—announces an incoming call, that input initiates a dopamine surge, or reward, in the brain. And the more those rings and vibrations reward us, the more we tend to repeat call-answering behavior. In fact, we have to continually repeat that behavior in order to experience the same reward.

Despite their occasional usefulness and value, many wireless devices tend to cause one glaring problem: They waste people's time and lower their productivity by rewarding those who engage in the movement of what I call *irrelevant minutiae*. No one has any *real* need to communicate with the same 3 or 10 people 200 times a day; the only value from doing so is the feeling of satisfaction that comes from the dopamine surge that's triggered.

Here's my challenge to you: Turn off your cell phone for a couple of hours each day and communicate in person with prospects about your business opportunity. If you think that this tendency to value an irrelevant minutiae accessory is not a problem, just pay attention for an hour to people in any mall, airport, or public place. You'll quickly notice that most addicts can pay attention to nothing else but their little screens. These technologies have the capability to poison your career—but only if you let them.

Any profession with the potential for unlimited income demands focus. That's why it is so important to turn off your wireless accessory for a specific amount of time each day, and work. I recommend going tech-free two hours a day. Turn off everything during that time. And don't be shocked if you feel anxious just thinking about doing so. That's the nature of addiction. It's called withdrawal. But you'll get over it—I promise.

Toxic Bomb 2: The Braying Mule

I use "mule" here to describe individuals who stand on the edge of their careers and bray at a new networker. They have nothing to contribute, nor do they have the courage to admit that they can't succeed without adhering to some sort of other-imposed structure. Mules can be dream-stealers, who stubbornly grunt negative comments at entrepreneurs, with the sole purpose of derailing their efforts. Some do so because they realize jealously that they lack the courage to even attempt relationship marketing.

When these individuals—whether they are strangers, family members, or friends—begin to bray, there's only one thing to do: Move on. Such people are beasts of burden who lack the thoroughbred qualities necessary to succeed without being constantly whacked with a stick. New independent business owners need to know how to recognize the mule bomb or they can easily be led astray by misconceptions.

A mule's problem is fairly straightforward: He or she needs structure and external motivation. These human mules respond to bosses, offices, quotas, and paychecks; they are extremely frightened by the notion of personal responsibility. Worse, they are especially jealous of those who dare to become racehorses. But instead of making the courageous decision to act like an entrepreneur and attempt to succeed through risk, sacrifice, and effort, mules often find comfort in hee-hawing at others who dare to dream.

Some mules believe that they can somehow elevate themselves by tearing down racehorses. The good news is, once new distributors are prepared to identify and avoid mules, they will never be dragged down by them.

Mules all seem to have one stubborn quality in common. Even if they know absolutely nothing about our industry, products, or specific companies, they are somehow against everything we promote. Mules don't have to be rational; they just need to be loud, negative, and abrasive. Their solitary goal is to stand in one spot and snort at everyone who comes within earshot.

Mules are also known to backbite their owners every chance they get. That's why new distributors must be warned about working around them: Even those who enroll and pretend to be interested can end up poisoning the whole team with negativity and backbiting.

Dream-stealers are a total waste of everyone's time. When you first encounter such negative people, the only option is to get away—quickly. They are not only incapable of succeeding in our industry; they actually take pleasure in causing chaos and inciting self-doubt among the players.

I grew up in the farmlands of Missouri and spent an entire childhood around mules; they are frustrating, stubborn animals. But what bothered me most about them had nothing to do with their willful behavior. To me, the worst thing about them was that you could never predict when one of them was going to bite you in the butt for absolutely *no* reason. (Perhaps they bite us because they are angered by the biological reality that they can't reproduce.) It's the same way with network marketing mules. As long as you're rewarding them with kind words, they'll eat out of the palm of your hand. But turn your back on a mule and watch what happens.

Stay with network marketing long enough and you'll find your thoroughbreds, trust me. Don't worry about all the mules you pass on the road. Mules can't help that they were born mules; and we must remember that we can never train them to be Kentucky Derby winners.

Toxic Bomb 3: The Neurologically Inadequate

According to those who have dedicated their entire careers to brain mapping and neurological medical studies, as many as 50 percent of all human beings are simply not cognitively hardwired to become entrepreneurs. They cannot—and *will* not—attempt network marketing.

Renowned Stanford psychologist Dr. Albert Bandura confirmed this notion for my partners and me when we spent an entire day with him in Palo Alto, California. We had his undivided attention for eight hours, during which we learned a great deal about what leads to personal wealth and self-efficacy. What we found most interesting was the conclusion from his research that success is not just about personal choice, but rather specific neurological hardwiring.

New networkers must realize two facts about prospects if they want to avoid setting off the neurological bomb. First, half of the people they approach cannot partake in network marketing. Second, most of those who can't will blame it on the profession, rather than admit to their own inadequacies and fears. Understanding those facts will allow new networkers to both anticipate and recognize what's *really* occurring when half the people they contact are immediately resistant or negative.

Here's how it works: Let's say we approach a woman who appears very talkative and outgoing. She may be wearing a Rolex or very expensive clothing, and appears as if she's experienced success. We may think she's a natural networker and therefore could be a tremendous addition to our team. Right? Not necessarily. She's a woman with a Rolex who may not be hardwired to ever perform tasks without structure or supervision. She may be a brilliant marketing representative with a Fortune 100 company who succeeds because of prescribed quotas, effective managers, a comfortable office, and an assigned territory.

We conclude that she's neurologically hardwired to succeed as an entrepreneur, because of her appearance and projected confidence. First, she doesn't know that she doesn't know how to be an entrepreneur—that's called *unconscious incompetence*. And even if she could fully accept her limitations, she wouldn't be able to admit them to a stranger, or even a friend. She will maintain her posture of self-assurance and poise to the bitter end; and to direct attention away from her own shortcomings, she will point out why pyramid schemes or home businesses are beneath her dignity and professionalism. She may actually sneer, or laugh off the approach nonchalantly.

And it doesn't always stop there. Occasionally, such naysayers feel the need to ridicule the networkers discussing these opportunities with them—as if doing so might somehow cover up their own character defects, fears, and inadequacies. More than all other land mines, new networkers must be prepared to sidestep this one, because it will inevitably surface when they're exposing a lot of prospects to the business.

As a new networker, accept that half the people you approach will say no simply because they can't operate within our business. Of the other half who are neurologically hardwired for our profession, most will be comfortable enough in their own occupations to decline your offer. Don't let those numbers and ratios upset you, because one good leader can make a big difference. That happened to me, and it has happened to everyone in my upline.

Toxic Bomb 4: The Social Network Meeting

A new class of networkers has emerged over the last few years. Not *network marketers*, mind you, just plain networkers. Because of the vast number of people who have found themselves outsourced and downsized during this period, many creative entrepreneurs decided that it would be profitable to launch meetings where those in similar circumstances could interact with one another and discuss matters of importance, like effective resume writing. They also realized that if they could bring in a few employers who might be looking for staff, they could draw even more people to these networking sessions.

It was actually a viable concept, in that it provided a way for meeting planners to gather together a group of vulnerable, unemployed individuals with the hope that they might make the connections necessary to find a job. It also made sense to companies looking for good people to send representatives to attend such meetings, because they had very little competition—potential employees usually outnumber employers at these meetings by about five to one. Like the proverbial beauty contest for five-year-olds, if you hold the pageant, people will come.

Next emerged networking gatherings for skilled entrepreneurs. Everyone who shows up to these meetings, with a stack of business cards in hand, has the opportunity to pitch their deal for three minutes to the whole room. The problem, however, is that most come with the same intention: to recruit people from other companies. And for some reason, everyone believes they are shrewd enough to recruit everyone else without being recruited themselves. Go figure.

One of your best moves in network marketing is to avoid this particular bomb at all costs. Don't be tempted to attend meetings to which people come to network with other networkers. Likewise, alert your new recruits to avoid those meetings like the plague.

Networking meetings were designed for the purpose of making money, not helping people. Leaders of these meetings do not awaken one morning with a sudden desire to facilitate a forum in order to help others make connections. In fact, as soon as an attendee gets a job, he or she never again has the need to come to another networking function. That's problematic for meeting planners who make money based on the number of those in attendance—not the number who quit coming.

I speak from personal experience here. I attended several of these meetings before I figured out how absurd they are. Never once did I recruit a winner who succeeded in my company. In short, if you want to meet great people who attend meetings with no hidden agenda, join a church or synagogue.

Toxic Bomb 5: The Product Expert

Some people believe that a thorough knowledge of their company's products or services is essential to success. And that's true in terms of using the products and acquiring testimonials from others who use them as well. You *must* believe in your products. However, the approach poses a problem when networkers go overboard, learn every tiny detail about a product or service, and then teach their own teams to do the same.

Product knowledge is absolutely essential. Yet you shouldn't become *so* obsessed with it that you spend your time learning each and every technical detail. Use the products, get your family using them, and experience the results. Testimonials about their efficacy are important; becoming an expert on how they are formulated is a distraction.

Not everyone is in the game to make piles of money. Some enter our profession to be trainers, while others want to be coaches, ministers, or counselors. I've met many men and women over the years who were perfectly content to form a small mastermind group whose members love their company's products and need a small social bonding experience each week. Network marketing provides the perfect vehicle for such people. They get to socialize with like-minded individuals and share personal stories and anecdotes about their valued products.

But what happens when those who are motivated by big checks find themselves recruited into a "product knowledge" group? They become frustrated, and either quit or rebel. It's problematic not only for the mastermind group, but it's also unfortunate for the new member who may desperately need to learn how to recruit large organizations and earn huge checks.

This land mine is paradoxical because it comes disguised as a formula for success. The concept of small weekly meetings that are exclusively product focused may be very important to the person who enters network marketing as a product user—one who has experienced dramatic product results—or joins without any desire for big checks. However, you don't need to know how the polysaccharides in a fruit are fractioned to penetrate the surface of the cellular membrane and force electrolyte absorption in each topical or sublingual administration of the juice your company is selling. You just need to know that the product works, is making a difference in many people's lives, and that networkers are earning huge incomes by moving the product through the distribution channel.

Here's the bottom line: It's generally understood that the products sold via network marketing are often superior to similar products sold in retail stores. They have to be for people to be willing to join our industry and recommend them to others. Countless individuals enlist in our profession for the purpose of achieving wealth and time-freedom. Those people cannot afford to waste their time learning the technical data necessary to become product experts; they realize that substantial payment results from recruiting and retailing, not from developing complex knowledge of a product. Yes, it's vital to be passionate about your products or services, but that passion must stem from the outcomes of use, not from knowledge of the intricacies of how they are made and/or work.

Customer acquisition is critical. The more people you recruit, the more customers you reach. In a legitimate network marketing opportunity, the larger the team, the more products wind up in the homes of end consumers. New distributors need to understand that the more time they spend in technical product knowledge sessions, the less time they will have to recruit new independent business owners; and the less time they spend recruiting, the smaller their group will remain. And smaller groups distribute fewer products to end users—which results in smaller checks to all independent business owners.

If the goal is large monthly checks, the action is simple: recruit more people. If the goal is socialization and nurturing, by all means study the products to your heart's content and schedule regular weekly product sessions.

Whether you join your company to experience a life-changing transformation by using its products, or you simply need to earn a greater income, those products will still be sold to folks who desperately need them. Thus, regardless of your motives, it's the business builders who help the most people. So avoid the product knowledge bomb; it will diminish your impact and income, and slow you down substantially.

Toxic Bomb 6: The Shortcut

Of all the toxic land mines in the network marketing field, number 6, the shortcut, is the most deadly because it is hidden *everywhere*— especially online. No matter how bright, successful, and experienced you become in our industry, this bomb will continue to block your progress until you make the firm decision to circumvent it.

There are no shortcuts to wealth through networking. Not one. Period. End of story. That doesn't keep people from sitting up all night arming this mine, to plant it in front of any vulnerable distributor who thinks he or she can purchase a shortcut to wealth. Sadly, many are just naive enough to believe in the shortcut fairy.

People might offer to sell you shortcuts that appear so brilliant and simple to execute that it seems only a fool would decline to take them—and, as it turns out, many a fool has fallen for them. In hopes of preventing you from becoming one of them, let me tell you about a few of the very toxic shortcut mines some teams have stepped on.

First, there was the infomercial shortcut. Next there was the health fair booth, followed by the fundraiser concept. Then there were the telemarketers and the wonderful phone room leads. And the corporate Christmas gift plan, and the "behind the counter at the retail pharmacy" plan. There were also the Primo network downline genealogy lists, and the Internet cartoon sites. After that, it was the $5,000 weekend Network Marketing camp and celebrity product endorsers. Not a single one worked. So remember, the shortest distance between two points is a straight line. The longest? A zigzag!

Network marketing requires that you establish a huge organization of dedicated entrepreneurs willing to work hard to move legitimate products or services to end users. There are *no shortcuts*.

Several years ago I offered a significant amount of cash to any networker who could build the same size group we had in the same amount of time using a shortcut. No one even tried to claim the prize. Why? Because they *knew* that there are no shortcuts. There are plenty of shortcuts for sale, of course; it's just that none of them work.

It's difficult to convince new people to avoid the shortcut land mine because, as their leader, you have no power over a volunteer force, and shortcut peddlers can be very seductive. Tell your team members to *only* follow the leaders in your company.

Remember this above all else: There are no shortcuts to dramatic wealth through networking. The only way to reap the benefits is to do the work required.

Toxic Bomb 7: Getting Stuck Getting Started

There's nothing wrong with preparation, and there's certainly nothing wrong with being organized. But to achieve wealth and success in our profession, neither is required to the extreme. Some people get stuck in getting started. Rather than going to work immediately, many new networkers will study, research, set up their computers and offices, listen to CDs, straighten paper clips, learn more, and organize still more, rather than recruiting or retailing.

Of course, there are plenty of companies hanging around the fringes of our industry selling systems to those who would rather study and speculate than execute. You can find many of them online. A simple Google search of our industry will provide a new networker with all the organizational tools he or she needs to waste money, time, and effort.

New networkers need to pay close attention to two facts. First, if organizational tools really helped to create wealth, those who developed them would be using them to earn millions; they wouldn't be selling them online. Second, new independent business owners need to be warned to avoid organizational systems that have zero value.

To repeat, there's nothing wrong with preparation and there's certainly nothing wrong with being organized. But wealth and success in our industry require neither.

Some of the most successful networkers I've ever interviewed were also the most disorganized. One mentor carried his entire list of leaders and their contact information on the back of two business cards, which he tucked under the cellophane cover of his cigarette pack. Although he had a company of more than 200,000 people, he didn't need to know how to reach more than 12, because they were the only "real" workers. Asked how he organized and kept track of his prospects, he replied, "What for? Either prospects sign up and go to work or they don't. I give them every opportunity. If they go to work, I put their home number on a card in my pocket. If not, I don't need their number!" An excellent point, indeed.

Countless men and women have called me over the years to help them figure out why they can't seem to build their networking businesses. Many have fabulous back offices, impressive websites, intricate recruiting and sorting follow-up techniques, remarkable lead lists, high-tech cell phones, and well-organized home offices. Many begin by telling me how methodical they are. They then lament that they've called for advice because none of their organizational strategies are working. Some become frustrated when I point out that they are *too* organized about the wrong things. Others understand when I suggest that they stop organizing and following up on prospects ad nauseum and instead start seeking new customers and business partners.

Network marketing is ideal for those who hate details, rules, structure, and organization. That's not to say that organized people can't succeed in our profession; but the truth is, many *don't*, because being organized requires a great deal of time and energy, which they could better spend recruiting and retailing. We get paid to work, not be efficient and organized.

Here's my recommendation: Try to recruit individuals who are *productive*, not necessarily organized. Once a person has all the big money and free time he or she needs, then it's fine to live an organized life. Teach your partners to resist the temptation to spend time organizing until they are earning at least $50,000 a month. Upon reaching that income level, they can afford to spend their entire lives focusing on the latest gadgets and supplies designed to keep themselves orderly.

To avoid the organizational bomb, give your new partners a task that requires zero organization. Suggest that they make a list of their top 25 potential business partners, and call you as soon as they're finished. If that process is too much for them, or a few days later they give you the excuse that they are almost "organized" enough to create the list, find new business associates. Making a list of your top 25 contacts requires zero organization

Toxic Bomb 8: The Fact Dump

Human beings are social animals; we love to communicate with others. That's one reason great trainers always caution new networkers to guard against overloading candidates with facts during the initial approach, as some will sabotage themselves by talking too much and for too long.

In network marketing, the fact dump bomb usually manifests in the first two steps: expose and present. New networkers often do a "data dump" of information on a prospect during the exposure step. Keep in mind that the purpose of this phase is to present exciting information *without* disclosing unnecessary facts, which will deter further investigation.

You do not need to reveal details during your initial approach. If you do, many of your prospects will never call you back because you've unwittingly set them up for a self-presentation. If they can Google your company, they will. They will do whatever they need to do to uncover all the facts they can and review them on their own. But that's the presentation step, and you need to be in control of that process so that you can answer questions and deflect objections stemming from prospect biases.

You must always caution new independent business owners against making this mistake, because the more information they dump on prospects in the exposure phase, the lower the chance that prospects will actually *join* their company. They also need to be aware that prospects will use very clever ways to get as much information as possible up front. They may act very interested, and frequently make leading comments like, "That sounds exciting. What's the name of your company?" Or, "This may be exactly what I'm looking for; tell me about your products!"

Some prospects will act offended when a networker won't provide them with more information at this point. I've heard comments like, "Look, I'm a very sharp businessperson. If you can't trust me with more information about your venture, I am just not interested. So, what's the product?" Don't fall for that ploy.

New distributors must be trained to watch for this land mine and to resist the temptation to dump information, which should be released during the presentation, rather than the exposure step.

There's another very good reason for adopting this strategy: Many prospects will attempt to direct the entire recruiting process. They realize that if they can take control from the get-go, and convince an independent business owner to do it *their* way, then that owner is not a leader. And though they will never admit it, prospects respect leaders who insist on an orderly process, rather than acceding to their requests.

Yes, we're social animals who love to talk. But the time to really talk business is during the presentation, not the initial exposure. If your team members reveal the presentation information during the exposure step, they will talk themselves right out of success by stepping on the fact dump bomb.

Toxic Bomb 9: The Banker

Everyone who tries to succeed—and especially those who *do* succeed—in this profession will, at one time or another, step on this bomb—you, too. But you'll suffer fewer injuries if you know about it from the very beginning. Keeping an eye out for and understanding this bomb can save you the loss of thousands of dollars.

Here's how it works: Let's say you are faithfully prospecting several people each day when you bump into a man who is very successful at what he does. He may be wealthy and completely happy with his current profession, but he is also very interested in what you are doing. He agrees to study any materials you can provide him. Naturally, you become excited because this man is obviously successful and well connected. It's obvious that he could be a real winner. Right? Maybe. Maybe not.

If this man offers to finance your efforts to build a group for him—or implies any combination of his cash and your effort—beware! That's the banker bomb. Remember, network marketing is about *effort*, not having capital to invest.

First, bankers are not leaders. They are businesspeople who have excess cash to invest in any venture that appears profitable. They seldom contribute more money than they can afford to lose, and zero effort. In other words, they're making no real sacrifice when they offer to finance you to build a group for them. And without a personal sacrifice, they never take the business seriously. Their motive is strictly a large return on investment—very large. In many cases, such a person will offer a big chunk of cash to partner with you fifty-fifty. But if you do all the work to create a lifetime income, and your banker partner does nothing but throw a little cash at you in the early stages, you will always resent him—and perhaps even wind up in court when you conclude how little he contributed.

Second, silent partners never remain silent for long. If, for example, you succeed in generating an income of a million dollars a year or more, your partner will usually decide to step into the limelight with you. He may even decide to abandon all his other ventures and go to work with you full-time. That can become a significant problem if he doesn't have a clue about building the business, and no one in the organization respects him. Bankers often believe that they are much smarter than others. So if your partner decides to jump in and help, you could be hooped—because even if he's an idiot, he owns half your enterprise.

Third, you begin to resent the guy because you feel cheated. All he did was front you $5,000 a month for a year. Now that the checks exceed $30,000 a month, you realize that this clown gets half the check for the rest of your life. You'll forget that in the early days

$5,000 a month was very significant, because now his return seems so unfair.

You might try to buy him out at that point; however, he will not consider this, and that can lead to horrible arguments, or even to court. You can't win in such as case, because a deal is a deal. Even if everyone in your organization is willing to stand up in depositions and swear under oath that you did all the work, half your check belongs to your partner—end of story.

So here's my suggestion. Don't take money from people who, as a result, could end up receiving half your check for life. Forget investment partnerships; you don't need cash to succeed. This business is about *effort*, not investment capital. I have seen fathers and sons, wives and husbands, and best friends since kindergarten wind up in litigation because they resented splitting large checks. If anyone offers you cash to build an organization, don't accept; don't step on the banker bomb. Politely decline—then go build your own team. Understanding how this bomb goes off could ultimately save you the loss of millions of dollars.

These explosive situations and counterproductive people will usually emerge in every networker's career. There will be others, but these are the most problematic. Go into partnership with those people and you'll waste a great deal of precious time. Networking partners are the key to your business, but not those whom you have to purchase, nor those who drain your emotional resources. We highly encourage you to study this chapter until you are familiar with every challenging personality type.

Chapter 12

SIMPLE TOOLS FOR DRAMATIC LEADERSHIP

Mark Yarnell

In this chapter I explore those ideas that are most important to leaders as they pursue their dreams and goals. I'll begin by stating a few assumptions:

- You're a member of a great company that offers an effective product or service.
- You have a strong desire for financial and time-freedom.
- The winds of change keep blowing harder, making it more difficult to lead effectively. Business as usual isn't cutting it anymore.
- You're ready to consider new ideas, concepts, perceptions, and strategies for developing the fifth network marketing competency: being an effective leader.

If those assumptions sound true, then this chapter is for you. Once you learn the concepts covered here, you'll be better equipped to recruit, lead, motivate, and serve your team. You'll learn the secrets of successful networking leaders and how to equip your team to stay motivated. I'll also alert you to the obstacles that frequently impede new independent business owners and weaken the resolve of those who've not yet developed key thinking skills and thought processes, or accessed tools to help them stay the course. You'll discover how to help these newcomers; or, if you're the one who's lost your way, you'll realize that it's never too late to correct your course, and find out how to do that.

There are specific skills and perspectives that will help you lead more effectively—and they're not difficult to learn. Leadership is a skill that every one of us can develop. In fact, each chapter in this book helps you become a better leader in some way. Collectively, the four of us have spent over a hundred years learning how to lead. It's not always been smooth sailing, and we've hit a few reefs along the way. However, we've also found, as Napoleon Hill wrote in his classic *Think and Grow Rich*, "Every adversity, every failure, every heartache carries with it the seed of an equal or greater benefit." Each time a wave swamps a good leader, he or she resurfaces and learns how better to survive the next one—provided the leader has the right attitude toward failure and struggle.

We've worked with many entrepreneurs who have asked, "How do I stay motivated and lead in spite of all of the obstacles I'm facing?" They want to know how to leap out of bed each day with passion—regardless of what happened yesterday—and inspire others to do the same thing. They want to know how to avoid sinking their boat in stormy seas of personal distractions and challenges. They tell us that just as they begin to set out in their business once again, they run into more rough waters. Sometimes, those waves are just too big, and too difficult to overcome. Many of those experiencing successes become exhausted from the effort of staying afloat and need to reenergize, while others struggle just to get started or stay with it. The ideas in this chapter will shed light on those issues of leadership.

Let's start with the first tool. In Chapter 8 Valerie discussed the importance of knowing your purpose, your "why." If you haven't already clarified this, do so now. Take the time right now to select from a number of possible driving forces for building your business.

This will prepare you to use this tool as a team leader, when you are working with new members and helping them get to the root of their purpose, or "burning desire." Ask them to put an asterisk (*) beside their three to five *most* important reasons for building their business. The ones listed here are possibilities; encourage newcomers to choose only those about which they're most passionate.

- Experiencing freedom—ultimately having the time to do what I want
- Enjoying the fun of a new challenge
- Having the ability to make a difference
- Distributing life-changing products to the world
- Spending more time with my family
- Funding my children's education
- Improving my home
- Paying off the mortgage
- Buying a better vehicle
- Looking after my/our health
- Traveling wherever I want, whenever I want
- Getting away from bosses; becoming my own boss
- Experiencing a greater sense of community and connection
- Making friends
- Practicing philanthropy
- Being allowed extra tax write-offs
- Working from home
- Being recognized for _____
- Retiring from my present job
- Other: _____

In addition to implementing this tool with new team members, you can use it as a guide to ask questions of your prospects to determine their "whys." Once you've zeroed in on exactly what they want and need, you can make your presentations more relevant to them. You must motivate others either by leading them into your business or convincing them to use your products or services. Talk with people; listen for their "whys" during each conversation with them.

Get to know them, and when the opportunity is right, invite them to look at your company. You may have a solution for them—especially if they are suffering from economic uncertainties.

Before examining the fears that paralyze some individuals, let's consider approaches we can all take to lead and motivate our partners. The most critical tack you can take as a leader is to respect your team members' aspirations. Some independent business owners love selling and retailing a lot of products, and will take the business no further than this. They have no desire to sponsor anyone, and earning a few hundred dollars a month is enough for them. If that's the case, don't hound them to recruit business builders, or you risk losing them. Simply let them know that sponsoring can make them extremely successful; don't try to transform them from a retailer to a recruiter if that's not what they want.

Many leaders fail to realize that one of their main responsibilities is to help shape the perspective of their team members. It's all part of motivating others to frame situations in a way that empowers them to do better. In doing so, you can shape a positive meme that spreads throughout your organization. For example, when distributors lose business partners, customers, or prospects, you can remind them that they're not psychologists, and it's not their job to try to understand why others behave as they do; to just accept their decisions and move forward with the plan. When things go wrong, help them look for the silver lining. Tell them it's both a blessing and a curse to be in a new company that, for instance, releases a marketing tool that contains spelling errors. The blessing is in the excitement and potential they are experiencing in the new venture; the curse is in the mistakes a new company is bound to make in its first few brochures or websites.

Always be on the lookout for emerging leaders. Stay closely attuned to what's happening in your organization. Bond with your promising associates; find out what's challenging them the most, and help them move through or around those roadblocks. Spend time with those who call you with good questions and stories that indicate they're moving forward. It's important to offer plenty of encouragement and find opportunities to provide "psychological paychecks."

The best teachers lead by example. They recruit and retail two hours a day. As such, your team will emulate what you do, not what you say. Even though you now have a team to support, you must continue to recruit and retail—and you must lead with your attitude. Anybody can be positive when things are going well, and challenges will certainly erode your emotional resilience. But as a leader, you must model attitude consistently. You don't have to be Pollyanna and ignore the reality of aggravating situations in order to demonstrate a positive mind-set; you do have to maintain a healthy perspective. Remember, a leader demonstrates what is possible.

The best coaching tools are those designed to prepare people to meet the inevitable challenges they will face—the most pressing of which is helping team members understand and cope with their fears. Many people avoid our profession because they're afraid; yet most of their fears are completely unfounded. And fears that become attached to unrealistic problems can develop into phobias. Remember, one of your roles as a leader is to help shape the perspectives of your team.

Prior to writing *Self-Wealth*, in the late nineties, my coauthors and I spent a day with Dr. Albert Bandera, the originator of social learning theory and the theory of self-efficacy, and learned from him an important fact about fears versus phobias: Fears are merely emotional concerns that arise as a result of legitimate dangers, whereas phobias are unrealistic fears that arise from perceived dangers that may not exist. The trick is learning the difference between the two. For example, many network marketers fear rejection, despite the fact that any perceived danger resulting from rejection is simply an unrealistic phobia. In 22 years of prospecting thousands of friends, family members, and strangers, not one person has ever hit me in the face or threatened to burn down my home. Some have laughed at me; others have made fun of our industry; and a handful have walked away from my approach and said nothing. Still others have attempted to argue with me about the ability to earn $30,000 a month. But never once have I experienced a truly serious outcome linked to rejection.

Again, keeping a healthy perspective is the name of the game here. Ask your team members, "Where's the danger in laughter, silence, criticism, and debate?" The answer is, *nowhere*. So let's view the fear trap from another perspective—because there is *zero* real danger in the process of recruiting new distributors or selling products, and because the rewards for attempting to do so are huge income and time-freedom.

What could cause anyone to become ensnared by fear? There are two reasons—and once you and your business partners understand them, a large part of the problem will disappear. We wrongly assume that:

1. We can control and manage false impressions others have of us and/or our business.
2. We are too fragile to face the reactions of others.

There's absolutely no danger attached to either of those possibilities—and rarely does anyone continue to think about you or your approach five minutes after you walk away.

Let's face facts: The fear trap in networking is nothing but a delusionary phobia, which can't—and *won't*—put anyone in actual peril. Yet this phobia prevents thousands of potential millionaires from achieving their dreams and goals. Those of us who have earned the big bucks are not calloused sociopaths immune to the pain of personal rejection. We are simply relational, critical thinkers who have concluded that we cannot manage the impressions and reactions of others; and even if we could, there's no money in it. The great news is there's no danger or pain in rejection. So if the downside is painless and the upside is prosperity, why let some silly phobia inhibit your potential success?

The views I am about to express about comfort zones are solely my own. To begin, I truly feel that too many opportunities are missed, relationships destroyed, and ethics undermined by the "comfort zone" mentality. Too many people are walking around in functional comas, multitasking merrily along the path of unproductive connectivity. And the worst part is that they're oblivious to the fact that they're *in* a comfort zone, multitasking rather than focusing on one thing and doing it well. The human brain is not hardwired to multitask. You cannot focus on A and B at the same time. Yes, you can shift your focus back and forth rapidly enough to delude yourself into thinking that you're performing both tasks well, but you can only truly concentrate on one endeavor at a time.

An obstacle becomes a trap when people become confined in repetitive, unproductive behavior. Let me close my discussion of the comfort zone traps with one final claim: North America's middle class is rapidly disappearing. According to the best minds in business, science, and technology, every one of us will either be ultrarich or ultrapoor within a mere 15 years. So, please, for your family's sake, find some passion or activity that will help you avoid the comfort zone traps. You must eventually escape these secure habits if you are to succeed. Start now; turn off the bells and vibrators, and get to work.

Yet another effective tool to help good leaders become great ones is to admit their shortcomings. An old cowboy saying from southwest Missouri, where I grew up, made sense to me as a kid, in spite of its grammatical incorrectness, and it still does: "There ain't no horse that can't be rode, and there ain't no cowboy who can't be throwed." Even champions aren't perfect. One of the most endearing personality traits of many of the great people I've met is their willingness to admit their imperfections. If you want to become a rich networker, stop all desperate pretending games and admit your deficiencies to the world. We all have them, and exposing them to others doesn't make you seem incapable; it makes you *relatable*.

In 1980, in the green room at a positive thinking rally, I was sitting with Dr. Norman Vincent Peale, the father of the positive thinking movement and author of *The Power of Positive Thinking*, and his wife. I found myself in complete awe of this great man. Though he was very old at the time, he'd lost none of the "power of positive thinking" that had brought him such renown. I couldn't resist the temptation to ask him if a man of his stature still had problems or ever did things for which he was sorry. He and his wife got a big laugh out of that one, before she proceeded to relate a priceless story by way of answering my question, while he sat by nodding and laughing.

Mrs. Peale explained that Dr. Peale was once a very messy man. Within 10 minutes of coming home from delivering a speech or church service, she said, the house would look like a tornado hit it. Shirts, underwear, pants, suits, and ties would be laying all over, while he escaped into his study to watch TV or read.

But before she could finish the story, Dr. Peale interrupted to point out that she had cured him of the problem. When I asked how, I thought they'd never stop chuckling. He said, "My lovely bride came home one day, got infuriated, and nailed my best sports coat to the floor. I try to hang everything up now!"

The perfectionism trap has ensnared countless networkers; but you don't have to be among them. You don't have to impress anyone with your brilliance. You don't have to learn the script perfectly, word for word. You don't have to dress for success (whatever that means). You don't need the latest wireless gadget to prove you're hip. You don't have to brag to your downline team about your "greatness." What you do need to do is to ask as many people as you can each day—as politely and sincerely as possible—if they will please buy your products or look at your business. Some will; some won't. Taking this action is the most important part.

Anyone can learn how to earn millions of dollars a year in this industry. But when you are taking home the big money and have all the free time you ever dreamed of, and everything in your life is absolutely wonderful, take it from me, you won't be one inch closer to perfection. So don't waste another moment striving for the unattainable.

Network marketing is similar in some respects to every other capitalist game: There are a handful of players and a multitude of spectators. But there's one major distinction: In our profession anyone can leave the bleachers, walk down to the field, and become a professional—at any time. It's all a question of choice and focus. Anyone can lead, inspire, and motivate.

First, you have to make the choice to become a leader, and then you have to ignore the spectators. I learned that fact in Scotland from one of the country's all-time greatest soccer players. He had joined my downline, and I had gone to Edinburgh to do some meetings for him; I had no idea until I arrived what a well-known celebrity he was. Everywhere we went, people asked for his autograph or a photo with him.

He took me to the empty stadium where he had played so many games in front of 35,000 screaming fans, and walked me onto the field. I was mesmerized by the size of the stadium, and asked him how in the world he could stay focused in front of all those shrieking soccer followers. "Let me show you something," he said, in response. "Let's walk around the field together."

We walked along a white line that marked the boundaries of the stadium field, and when we had come to the end, he made this incredibly meaningful statement: "All that matters happens inside those lines. When I run out onto this field, I focus on absolutely nothing but what is happening inside that rectangle. During the entire game, nothing else exists." I got it. And I can honestly say that his remark can be applied exactly to the game of networking.

Everybody wants to win, but few are willing to turn pro, and still fewer are willing to focus on the only two ways to win—recruiting and retailing. It's a small field with clear boundaries. Recruit and retail, and you score. Babysit noncommitted people and you might as well be right back up in the bleachers drinking beer and yelling at the players.

It would be wonderful if weekend golfers could just decide to turn pro and purchase a PGA card. But they can't. It would be wonderful if Microsoft executives could decide to become co-chairmen of that company and earn as much as Bill Gates; but they can't. I'd love to drive a Formula 1 car in just one Indianapolis 500; I can't. But in 1986, I was facing repossession of my car and foreclosure on my home; I was broke and in debt. One year later, I was earning over $30,000 a month and living in a ski chalet in Aspen. I think that makes the network marketing industry the greatest game on earth.

If you want to really serve your team, demonstrate what's possible—every single day. The most overarching theme in leadership is the importance of "walking the talk," demonstrating leadership by doing what you say you're going to do and what you're asking others to do. Credibility is the number-one attribute of a leader. You're the leader, the recruiter, and the motivator—not the manager. In fact, when you stop leading and start managing, you are hooped—and your group is finished. The greatest cause of failure among those who have remarkable leadership skills is the unfortunate tendency to fall victim to the management trap, because telling people what to do is so much easier than *demonstrating* what's possible.

Although the leadership and personal motivation tools I've described here may seem obvious and simple, they are highly significant. Many will read them and think, "I know that." Winners will *apply* them.

Chapter 13

SERVANT LEADERSHIP

For Lasting Loyalty and Personal Satisfaction

Derek Hall

The greatest blessings I've experienced in my life have come from serving others and seeing the joy and excitement that comes to them when they succeed in achieving their goals. It's addictive to contribute to someone else's accomplishments. Once you start to see the results of your personal efforts on someone else's behalf, you just can't get enough of it.

No one has ever been successful in or accumulated wealth from a network marketing business without also creating wealth for his or her colleagues in the organization. It is simply the nature of the business model. Your income will grow exponentially the more you concentrate on making others successful and increase your efforts on their behalf. Truly, this is a business model that can produce untold wealth by way of helping and serving others.

Conversely, if you are not willing to practice servant leadership in your network marketing company, you will never reach the level of success you are aspiring to, not even in this very lucrative business model.

I remember an event that took place years ago, when my two sons were about 11 and 13 years old. It was the beginning of summer, and in Utah where we lived at the time, the weather is very dry and hot at that time of year. Homeowners commonly use swamp coolers to cool their homes. A neighbor of ours, a single mom, had no clue how to service her cooler, and no money to hire someone to do it for her. So my boys and I climbed up on the roof of her home, replaced the pads in the unit, turned on the water, and otherwise readied it for the summer. The entire process took less than an hour.

After we finished and were walking back to our house that morning, one of my boys made a comment that has stayed with me for over 30 years. He said, "Dad, I feel great after doing that work; I have a really warm feeling in my chest." I was impressed that both of my sons were experiencing—and acknowledging—the fulfillment that comes only from serving another person. They were feeling exactly the way I was, and for doing what I considered to be a menial task for a friend and neighbor, who considered it to be a monumental favor.

BACKGROUND OF SERVANT LEADERSHIP

The concept of *servant leadership* is not a new one; however, it is only within the last 40 years or so that it was given a name. The term was coined by Robert K. Greenleaf in his essay "The Servant as Leader," published in 1970. In it he says:

> The servant-leader *is* servant first . . . It begins with the natural feeling that one wants to serve, to serve first. Then conscious choice brings one to aspire to lead. That person is sharply different from one who is *leader* first, perhaps because of the need to assuage an unusual power drive or to acquire material possessions. The leader-first and the servant-first are two extreme types. Between them there are shadings and blends that are part of the infinite variety of human nature.

I know of many organizations, my own among them, that have made the concept of servant leadership the core of their cultures.

Doing so has revolutionized their human resources management to become more than the process of hiring and firing. Consequently, employee turnover at them is a very minor factor in the human relations equation, for the simple reason that it becomes virtually nonexistent.

No matter what you call it, divorcing yourself from the need to self-aggrandize, and instead focus on others, is necessary if you want truly to succeed. Those who have made a name for themselves in a network marketing business will tell you that the art of creating residual income involves doing all you can to make the members of your downline organization successful. The more successful they become, and the more income they earn, the more residual income you will accrue. So study this chapter closely because its message is crucial to your success as a networker.

Genuine servant leaders are successful entrepreneurs, and in this chapter I tell you exactly why and how. In doing so, I challenge you to produce another example of this business model that can generate millions of dollars in residual income for all involved, based on your ability to serve and motivate the rest of your team. I assure you, there's no greater reward than watching the people who work for you enjoy success, while you are accumulating wealth as well. If you do things for the right reasons in your networking business, wealth will follow. As the Viennese psychologist Alfred Adler wrote in his book *What Life Should Mean to You,*

> It is the individual who is not interested in his fellowmen who has the greatest difficulties in life and provides the greatest injury to others. It is from among such individuals that all human failings spring.

My good friend Jerry Campisi is a wonderful example of someone who has learned the real value of servant leadership. Jerry has been involved in network marketing for almost 30 years and currently serves as a master distributor in a network marketing company; as such, he has tens of thousands of distributors within his organization. He began his networking career with Nu Skin, an extremely successful network marketing company that does business around the world. Jerry has made tens of millions of dollars in the three decades he has spent in networking, and in that time he has come to embrace the servant leadership philosophy and practices it daily.

The leaders in Jerry's organization look to him as a mentor, and more importantly as an expert; he remains on call 24 hours a day to assist in any way he can. It's clear that Jerry enjoys the rewards of helping the members of his team achieve their goals. He makes himself available for three-way calls at the drop of a hat, and provides the nurturing required by his many fledgling distributors as they begin their network marketing journeys. He is quick to remind the newest networkers that they will never find another business model in which they will work so hard for so little reward for the first two to three years, and then work so little for so much in the ensuing years.

Jerry also teaches to lead using servant leadership principles, and requires his new leaders to, in turn, "pay it forward." He is, and has been, tremendously successful because he understands the essence of servant leadership.

CHARACTERISTICS OF SERVANT LEADERSHIP

Larry C. Spears, who served as president and CEO of the Robert K. Greenleaf Center for Servant Leadership for 17 years, has extracted a set of characteristics that are central to the development of a servant leader. They are:

- Listening
- Empathy
- Healing
- Awareness
- Persuasion
- Commitment to the growth of people
- Building community

Every one of these characteristics is an essential component of the network marketing model.

Listening

Until just a few years ago my hearing had been fairly reliable; but then my wife began to complain that I didn't always hear her when she was speaking to me. It seems I was missing a lot of what she was saying, and it was beginning to be a problem for her. I mentioned this to some of my male friends who are of the same "vintage" and discovered that this problem is quite common among men of my age—it may even be approaching epidemic proportions. I did some additional research, including further interviews with men of my age (which produced a lot of laughs), and had several soul-searching conversations with my wife about this problem. I came to realize that it wasn't my hearing that was deteriorating; it was my ability to listen carefully and attentively.

My point in sharing this personal story is that servant leaders must be extremely practiced in the art of listening. As Henry Ford once said, "If there is any one secret of success, it lies in the ability to get the other person's point of view and see things from that person's angle as well as from your own."

I would even go as far as to say that the skill of listening well is a God-given talent—one that we all have but that few master, and thus, are able to capitalize on. Listening attentively is crucial for anyone who desires to maximize their servant leadership skills. That said, it's not just about listening with your ears. As we make eye contact with someone we are sitting next to or across from, we send and receive nonverbal signals that are as important—if not more so—than the spoken words exchanged between you. We all learn through life's experiences that it's not so much what we say; it's *how* we say it. True servant leaders understand this concept completely, and demonstrate it in all that they do.

Empathy

A true servant leader doesn't stop at listening carefully to others; he or she also seeks to understand how they feel, to express empathy. This ability is priceless in a business environment. A professional leader who understands the concerns of his or her team members will excel, because he or she will be able to spot possible obstacles early and remove them before they become insurmountable. Leaders must raise themselves up to a level from which they can perceive potential problems among their fellow stakeholders. Otherwise, they may fail not only as influential leaders, but quite possibly will damage their business permanently, as well.

The ability to empathize with people you interact with is empowering for both parties, which is why it is such an important tool for establishing what I call a "legacy business." Seasoned network marketers get to know the leaders within their organization; they work side-by-side with them in order to understand what needs to be done to achieve the individual, as well as collective success, all are striving for.

Healing

This component of a servant leader's character is closely related to empathy, in that it requires leaders to align themselves with those they are trying to assist or advise.

Servant leaders heal by resolving issues among team members and acting as the liaison between parties in contention, in an effort to mitigate conflicts. Servant leaders who perfect this skill gain the trust and loyalty of all who work for and with them. Consequently, the professional environment is devoid of fear, and all involved typically feel empowered in their positions. The network marketing business can be very competitive, and so brings with it a high probability of conflict. A servant leader must, therefore, learn how to intervene effectively to alleviate and eliminate such conflicts in such a way that all parties feel healed.

Awareness

By now it should be apparent that to excel as a leader you must remain aware of all that's happening around you. It's as simple as that. If you are disconnected, how can you expect to know how others around you feel, and get a sense for the kind of guidance they need? How can you mitigate a problem if you are out of touch? There are a variety of ways to accomplish this important function.

Network marketing leaders rely on the members of their business to generate sales that accrue to all involved in the venture. They plan weekly meetings for the purpose of bringing members together to discuss what works and what doesn't. This allows leaders to develop an understanding of both the possible paths and obstacles to success, and serves to guide them in working with all their team members to solve a problem or capitalize on an opportunity.

Only when leaders really listen, and hear, what others tell them, can genuine and enduring communication take place. My wife likes to say that one of the greatest illusions about communication is that it has already occurred. Just because we have said what it is we want to communicate doesn't necessarily mean that we did a good job, that the recipient understood our message.

Persuasion

All successful men and women understand the value of being persuasive. As teenagers, we quickly learned the importance of persuading our parents to, for example, let us take the car, or stay out later than our curfew. As adults we realize that the art of persuasion is a marvelous tool that can help us as we go through life and progress in our chosen careers. More important than having power and authority is learning how to *use* them for the good of all concerned.

Fortunately, there is more than one effective way to exert power and authority. *Unfortunately*, many choose to exert what I call *position power*—more commonly called the authoritarian approach. We've all heard words to the effect: "I don't care what you think; I'm in charge here and we're going to do it my way." This approach works, often very well; but I contend it should be used only as a last resort. Those on the receiving end of such a declaration come to know very early that what they think doesn't matter much to the person making it. Such a leader is not a good candidate for the Servant Leader of the Year Award.

A much better way to accomplish what needs to be done than to take this "in your face" tack is to use *personal power*. This approach compels individuals to take advantage of their inherent gifts, talents, and skills to convince others to do what needs to be done, or to help them see an issue from your perspective. By using your personal power as a leader, those you are working with won't feel threatened; rather, they will feel they are participants in the solution and partners in the process. Thus, they will develop a sense of empowerment themselves, because their leader is asking for their input and advice.

For years I have thought of this concept as "getting someone to do what needs to be done without their realizing they are doing it." Being tactful and diplomatic is, perhaps, the most crucial of all the servant leader components, as it distinguishes clearly the move away from the traditional authoritarian approach, and to the servant leadership management style.

This chapter makes it clear how a softer, more laid-back approach—one that encourages the use of *personal power*—can enable you to interest your warm-market prospects and convince them to listen to a presentation about your new venture.

Commitment to the Growth of People

Servant leaders believe that they are rewarded both emotionally and financially by making others successful. They have faith in others and embrace the principle that they are not above anyone else; only that they have different titles, responsibilities, and job descriptions.

Servant leaders also care for their constituents, and are driven to see them succeed. As such, they provide professional continuing education, as well as personal coaching and training, as their personal schedules permit.

Dr. Taylor Hartman, author of the bestselling book *The Color Code* has been my personal friend, teacher, and confidant for over 20 years. Here's how he explains this characteristic of leaders:

> Helping others feel important enhances the quality of our
> own lives as well. We create a win-win relationship when

we are able to get over ourselves long enough to listen and make others feel heard.

He goes on to describe "getting over yourself" using this priceless analogy:

If you own a dog (or better said, have a dog who owns you), you live with the master of making other people feel important. What a natural role-model! Do you realize that a dog is the only animal that doesn't have to work for a living? A hen has to lay eggs, a cow has to give milk, and a canary has to sing, but a dog makes his living by giving you nothing but love. We have a sheltie named Dusty who just lives for my son, T.J. Every day when T.J.'s school bus is about to arrive at our house, Dusty slips out the back door and runs to the bus stop to wait for him to step off the bus.

How does he do that? How does he know the time? He doesn't have a watch. Yet, every school day, out he goes. Dusty intuitively knows what all dogs know—that you can make more friends in two minutes by being genuinely interested in other people than you can in two years by trying to convince other people to be interested in *you*.

Servant leaders check in often with those they lead as a way of opening the door to anyone receptive to being tutored by them. They learn the names of those they lead, and use them often in their presence to establish trust and inspire the loyalty that stabilizes the team. Servant leaders establish common ground with their team members, to set the stage for the development of trust and loyalty, and to let everyone know that they are contributing to the success of the enterprise.

Building Community

When I think of this trait, what comes immediately to mind is the development of an organizational culture. Building a community culture is second nature to a servant leader; and it is paramount to the development of a loving and caring environment where all can grow, enjoy success, and earn a living together. A community culture is one that encourages team players, or employees, to take calculated risks based on solid research. Servant leaders welcome such risk-taking, and when it pans out, reward it accordingly.

Servant leaders also recognize that failure is inevitable along the road to success, and are extremely understanding when risk taking ends in disappointment. I call this aspect of community culture "permission to fail." This empowering concept eradicates the fear of failure among team members, thus allowing for the free flow of ideas and concepts—which ultimately drives the success of the organization.

The culture of servant leadership is not a "program of the month"; it is a lifetime commitment that organizations and individuals must make if they are to adopt a new paradigm for dealing with one another. In my own experience as the leader of more than one commercial enterprise, and thousands of employees, I have seen teams of employees transition their thinking, and in the process create a more forgiving and, frankly, more credible work ethic by doing so. This attitude, and the kind of culture in which it can thrive, leads to elevated customer relationships, as well as enhanced loyalty and trust in corporate leadership. In the end, we tend to treat others as we ourselves are treated—good or bad.

Another way to express this paradigm shift is to say that team members can better relate to the culture and adopt it as their own while gaining a deeper understanding of the overall business strategy. Your networking team members will come to appreciate their own personal worth in the organization and, therefore, be more willing and able to contribute to its overall success.

Likewise, leaders define themselves by the way team members regard and treat them—because leaders need love, too. They garner a great deal of respect by, literally, turning the traditional pyramid organizational chart upside down. Instead of the base serving the few at the top, the reverse occurs; the few at the top serve the many at the base. After all, as previously stated, a network marketing company is no more a pyramid than any other corporate structure.

However, this upside-down pyramid is revolutionary when implemented under the servant leadership model.

HOW SERVANT LEADERSHIP APPLIES TO YOUR BUSINESS

By now you may be thinking, "This all sounds good, but what does it have to do with network marketing in general, and to my home-based business specifically?" That's a great question. And here's the answer.

The business of buying and selling is nothing more than the act of determining who you trust and believe. Each of us makes a series of value judgments as we watch commercials on television and become attracted to a product or service. We ask ourselves, "Is the product or service worth the price?" "Does it look like it will meet my needs?" "Is it manufactured by a reputable company, one I can trust?" Many other questions will crop up during this process, in a fraction of a minute—and be answered just as quickly.

We take a risk every time we purchase anything; and depending on the cost of the product or service, the risk can be monumental or miniscule. Of course, the risk is far greater when we are buying big-ticket items such as houses or cars than when we are deciding whether to purchase a pair of sunglasses or a small household appliance. Yet, in either case, we are weighing the trust factor: Can we *trust* the manufacturer, or the sales representative sitting in front of us?

The beauty of the network marketing model of distribution is that you are often sitting across a table or desk from an individual who has much to gain if he or she accepts your offer to join your business. But the downside is huge if the opportunity is misrepresented. All successful professional networkers understand the value of living and breathing the servant leadership mentality and culture. When you, too, immerse yourself in the concept of serving others, you will do whatever it takes to convince the person you're recruiting to become your business partner. You not only bring a financial opportunity to that individual; his or her success accrues to you, as well.

As consumers have become better educated, the days of talking heads and slick shysters have all but passed. We study long, and research issues hard and deep to find out if there are any flaws in an opportunity before we take the leap. We have become very savvy, thanks in part to the Internet and the easy access we now have to unlimited data. We also read labels more carefully these days, and are always on the lookout for things to avoid—especially when it comes to products we take into our bodies.

True servant leaders will thrive in the world of network marketing. More than any other type of leader, they will reap the benefits of the growing distribution channel that those of us in the business affectionately call *relationship* or *network marketing*.

YOUR MARKETING TOOLKIT– AFTER THE FIRST 90 DAYS

Advanced Networking Strategies

Before delving into the advanced strategies in Part III, let's touch on the subject of technology. As we all know, technology continues to change at warp speed. Today's wireless gadgets quickly become tomorrow's recycled trash. None of these tools will stop evolving long enough for a professional networker to build his or her entire strategic program around them without appearing "out of touch" within a very short time. That's the downside. The upside is that technology allows us to expedite the flow of information to a much larger number of prospects in a much shorter period of time.

However, while some folks believe they can use text messages and social media to build relationships, network marketing has always functioned on the concept of *relationship marketing*. We believe that relationships can be much deeper and more trusting when people communicate face-to-face; that there will always be a need to form actual social groups, to interact in person or on the telephone in real time. If technology ever replaces face-to-face, word-of-mouth, or relationship marketing, network marketing will cease to exist very shortly thereafter. Why would a company pay independent business owners half of every dollar to recruit and retail if they can move their products and services through distribution channels and pay minimum wages to a handful of people?

Don't misunderstand; this is not to denigrate or underestimate the advantages offered by websites, wireless devices, and the countless other new technologies. We count on them to enhance the speed, reach, and effectiveness of information dispersal. At the same time, we do not believe technology can ever replace genuine social contact or word-of-mouth advertising. We might even go so far as to say that our profession's greatest advantage is that machines can never replace us. In other words, networkers are safe from outsourcing, downsizing, and replacement by technology. We aren't standing on an assembly line tightening bolts, or sitting in an office cubicle crunching numbers; we are human beings talking to other human beings. So, yes, technology provides us with some wonderful tools, but, no, they're not replacements for you and me—and they never will be.

By all means, utilize social networking to reach out; generate connections with new people and reunite with some from your past. But reserve social media for connecting, rather than for exposing and presenting your business. Develop relationships, collect contact information, and then *speak to people directly*. This is how genuine relationships are built.

In Chapters 14 and 15 you'll learn several more marketing strategies to help you perform at the very top of your game.

Chapter 14

THE $100K TOOLKIT

Mark Yarnell

The tools that make it possible to earn $100K a month in network marketing are so obvious that when you point them out to people they will often seem embarrassed that they hadn't considered them. (Of course, it's never a good strategy to ridicule prospects for missing the obvious.)

Most of us have seen television shows in which average people have paid a few bucks for some ugly works of art, only to discover that antique experts regard them as treasures and value them at obscenely high prices. While it's always possible to become wealthy by being lucky, productivity coupled with wisdom are generally much more likely to result in financial security. This chapter provides the wisdom and the tools you need to hit the ball out of the park; the productivity is up to you.

TOOL 1: UNILATERAL FOCUS

None of us has ever met anyone who has risen to the very top of any human endeavor as a result of part-time effort. Can you think of a part-time Super Bowl quarterback? How about a surgeon, CPA, corporate leader, politician, or professor, who only has to work every so often to make it to the top of his or her profession? Most of us take comfort in the fact that there are numerous laws on the books designed to protect us from part-time dabblers. After all, who wants to turn their assets over to a part-time stockbroker, or save money by undergoing heart surgery performed by a part-time surgeon who is assisted by amateur nurses? When was the last time a part-time golfer won the Masters, or a part-time racecar driver won the Daytona 500? Ever hear of a part-time marathon runner winning an Olympic Gold Medal, or some nameless Wikipedia contributor writing an international best seller?

The simple point I'm making here is this: People who excel at what they do focus on the one endeavor until they *become* great at it. The essence of network marketing is no different from any other field. In fact, given our ability to earn huge amounts of income, it may actually be *more* unilaterally focused than other professions. I've racked my brain, and I still can't think of one person who has entered this profession and achieved dramatic, full-time income by making a part-time effort—not one. Occasionally, a man or woman has started part-time, made a big pile of money by recruiting a handful of good people, then made the choice to quit his or her day job and move forward in our industry full-time. Others have made the choice to work in our business full-time after a couple of part-time years, during which they were able to replace their previous job income. But no one achieves and sustains the huge checks by multitasking or focusing on a dozen things at once.

I am not suggesting that you attempt to talk your people into burning their bridges and working full-time from month one. That's not your role. I do recommend, however, that you take a long look in the mirror. Are you trying to be a part-time leader? If so, do you really think people are going to overlook your lack of focus? Are prospects going to join your team and be satisfied with your part-time example? Are you working part-time because in your heart of hearts you have witnessed your company take actions that worry you, like downline (the team under you) switching or making changes in the compensation plan? Do the products lack scientific validation or patents to protect them? Does your spouse refuse to support you in your efforts? Are you genuinely afraid that you lack the personal motivation to succeed? Is your upline leader unethical, incompetent, or missing in action? If that's the case, have you searched as many levels above you as possible and still could find no one to work with you? Are some newer people in your company leaving full-time jobs because they are earning a full-time income through your venture?

Your reasons for part-time involvement are inconsequential, since one excuse is as good as the next. But here's what I know: The number one tool in the arsenal of all wealthy networkers is *unilateral focus*. Eventually, we must each face the big question: Am I willing to go full-time and give this opportunity the effort it warrants? It's okay if your answer is no. Just realize you will never *truly* know whether you could have earned $100K a month by following in the footsteps of those of us who have given network marketing our unilateral focus. Part-timers seldom — if ever — luck out and "somehow" make $100K a month.

TOOL 2: THE CROSS-PLATFORM EXPOSURE IMPLEMENT

As you've already learned, prospects must undergo several steps before arriving at a decision. The first — the exposure step — is the most critical. Prospects must be compelled to perform due diligence. You will need to grab their attention and motivate them to investigate your business thoroughly. The sharpest arrow in your recruiting quiver is a *cross-platform implement*, a short, compelling narrative that's available in every conceivable delivery system. You will need to provide provocative, informative, and motivational information via a tool, which you should make available in multiple forms.

And when you meet people face-to-face, be prepared to hand them a recorded exposure tool. If you meet them online or over the telephone, have the same information available on a website and send a link to it immediately. Make each exposure tool available in every conceivable format so that you can give prospects the information as soon as possible.

There are two kinds of exposure tools: generic and specific. You'll find an example of a generic one at www.yournewbusiness-plan.com. I recommend that you or your team leader create either a specific or generic implement, as this tool will become a critical component for anyone who wants to earn the big money. The more effective CDs you hand out or websites you refer people to, the more money you will make, assuming that you have immediate access to the next tool—the validation master.

TOOL 3: ACCESSIBLE VALIDATION MASTER

Most "big-money" networkers have one strategic advantage over other independent business owners; but some do not want to discuss this asset because it tends to diminish their own feelings of greatness. There are great master networkers in every legitimate network marketing company. Those individuals are exceptionally skilled at selling, motivating, and closing new prospects. They've made the big bucks, heard every conceivable objection, and know how to handle each one. Prospects literally have no way to rebut them. Somewhere in your upline, there is a man or woman who will benefit from your success. Seldom are any of us personally sponsored by one of these masters. Usually, we are way below them in the downline. The trick is to track upline until you find a master who will do three-way calling with you—referred to as the *validation step*.

It is critical to gain access to at least one master distributor, otherwise, you're likely to find yourself in a world of trouble. Why? Because every great networker was a lousy networker first—and you are no exception. The greatest benefit of our profession is that it allows us to serve an apprenticeship under a master networker. Take that away and it's all just a crapshoot. This is not to say that new independent business owners will not be able to succeed unless they have a master to call on; it does say that their odds of rising to the top will be greatly diminished if they don't take advantage of this opportunity. That's why so many owners of upstart companies are willing to pay master distributors huge signing bonuses to come on board. Their abilities and wisdom are, simply, invaluable.

If no one in your upline is both successful and accessible, you will be at a very serious disadvantage. That's the hard truth of the matter—though I assure you, you will not be told that in most other books about this industry. In fact, if such a person is not in place, it should be a deal breaker, because it signals several factors, each of which is a significant problem. First, there's nobody making the big money. Second, there's nobody making the big money who has the desire to coach those who need it. Or, third, the leaders are all playing the ego game of "you're not worthy enough yet to deserve my valuable time." Not one of those reasons is valid. (You might want to show this chapter to those who refuse to coach you and see if they change their minds. If not, it may be time to cut your losses and find a real deal with the kind of support and partnership you need.)

TOOL 4: THE WOY

It's amazing how few people understand the "worked on you" (WOY) factor. The reason so many great people who could and should have made big money in this business quit in frustration is because they forget what got them so interested. For some reason, many will get all excited about something that is said about the products, team and company—so excited that they sign up, buy a kit, and make a list of people to contact. Many learn a script and start immediately making contacts. After a few calls they forget what initially "worked on them." At that point, feeling somewhat rejected, they switch systems and begin pitching an entirely different concept than the one that originally impressed them. That's when everything begins to unravel.

Here's a real-life example: Bob was downsized by his corporation and spent a couple of months looking for another position, but couldn't seem to find anything because no one was hiring. He then got a call from his CPA, who proceeded to introduce him to a ground-floor network marketing launch. Bob needed to make big money, so after doing some significant due diligence, he joined the company, started taking the products (health care), and became completely enamored with their therapeutic value. He stopped having headaches and started sleeping like a baby, for the first time in 20 years. Next thing you know, Bob has created a website and blog with the goal of enticing a huge number of customers to experience the product benefits.

What was Bob's error? Simple. He forgot about WOY—he forgot what *worked on him*—and shifted his recruiting strategy from big money and free time to headache cures and insomnia relief—a serious mistake.

Remember this tool: Stick with what worked on you. Only some people suffer from bad headaches, whereas most folks desperately want financial security.

Remember, if you joined a company for reasons like Bob's—that is, big money and free time—don't then try to become a lay doctor (or fitness guru, or fashion expert, or whatever the case may be). Stay focused on the approach that *worked on you*! That is definitely the one most apt to work on others.

TOOL 5: INSIGNIFICANT AVOIDANCE STRATEGY

Several years ago a small group of industry leaders and trainers decided to perform what they called a "network marketing autopsy." Their goal was to accumulate a list of professionals who had quit our industry in their first few months without really giving it a fair shot. They wanted to determine whether they could identify specific causes of failure. They found one: fear of insignificance. Simply put, one of the primary laws of human nature is that we all have an honest need to feel valued, personally relevant, and significant. Men or women who have distinguished themselves in particular fields have enjoyed a great deal of peer respect. Often, that respect carries more importance to such individuals than money.

Consider the following scenario: Nancy owns a highly profitable franchise, but the economy has slowed her company's growth. She begins to look around for alternative income options when a good friend introduces her to a promising new network marketing company. Nancy does a significant amount of research on the firm and ultimately decides to purchase a kit and get started. Her upline coach tells her to make a list of her best 25 contacts, which she does. Then, armed with little more than raw enthusiasm, Nancy starts calling the people on her list—best friends first— people who respect her as a successful franchise owner. Several of them have absolutely no interest in network marketing; but instead of treating her with the respect to which she is accustomed, they reject her approach utterly. Consequently, for the first time in a decade, Nancy's self-esteem suffers a major "hit." The last thing she wants or needs now is to feel marginalized by friends. After a few calls in the first few days, Nancy is crushed by feelings of insignificance and lack of respect, and she quits.

Nancy's case is not unusual. It is repeated time and again in this industry. What's the solution?

It's to teach new independent business owners to stay away from their close friends and relatives *until* they have practiced on contacts who don't mean as much to them. Nancy should have been instructed to contact her second-tier friends and contacts first, especially those she doesn't care much about recruiting. If they sign up, great; but she certainly shouldn't go after her potential best players at the outset. The reason is that Nancy, like all new networkers, needs experience answering objections. Everyone has common, boilerplate arguments about our industry they're ready to voice at the beginning of this process. Stereotypical biases are viral in professional networking.

Here's something else you must keep in mind: All new leaders believe they have at least two friends who will sign up immediately on their front line and help make them wealthy. What they don't realize is that even their closest friends will respond initially by throwing out two or three arguments—generally, ridiculous ones. The Nancys of the world are not prepared for those arguments; they just assume that their friends have such respect for them that they'll jump right into the deal and go to work. Instead, they resist, poopoo network marketing, and make the new networker feel worthless, sometimes for the first time in years.

So here's the strategy: Make certain that Nancy does not approach her best warm-market friends until the second week of practice, after she's faced and surmounted a few objections. Otherwise, she'll walk away from this business convinced that the very people she assumed would help her succeed and make her wealthy couldn't care less about being her partner.

Nancy's assumption that her charm and brilliance would be enough to recruit her best friends was, sadly, incorrect. She—like all new networkers—needed to prepare herself for the initial reactions of friends *before* she approached them.

Valerie and I have great friends who have watched us earn millions in this industry. They invite us to social events, and love us immensely. But when we bring up a new networking company, they act like cornered wharf rats. So clearly, this is not the place to start.

TOOL 6: THE INSURANCE POLICY

You don't need to recruit people the first time you meet them. But you *always* want to plant a seed that will eventually sprout and prompt virtually any prospect to call you back when the time is right. Many people you approach will either be in a network marketing company or will have been in one recently. That means they're either angry because they just failed, or pretending to be happy in their current company, even if they are miserable. Don't try to reason with them. All prospects will eventually be in a position to quit what they're doing and change companies. Tell everyone you meet that you want to be their insurance policy. Here's my script:

James, I'm glad you are involved in my profession. Please remember one thing. You now have an insurance policy, and that insurance policy is me. If you ever find yourself earning less than you're worth, or anyone in your company lies to you or refuses to live up to your values, call me. I'm in a great deal and I'll always be here for you. Promise to call me first if you are ever in need of change.

Use the *insurance policy tool* on everyone you meet. The average person changes jobs every 3.6 years, for a wide variety of reasons. Plant the seed in the brain of every prospect that you are their exit strategy.

Now you have them, the secret tools of many wealthy networkers. All are calculated to help you earn $100K a month. They work—and they work very effectively.

Chapter 15

THE ULTIMATE REJECTION-FREE RECRUITING STRATEGIES

Mark Yarnell

A s pointed out previously, fear of rejection often causes network-ers to freeze. Even though we're all aware that rejection doesn't involve physical danger or cause injury, some people dread it so much that they become paralyzed and can't move forward in their work and lives. But what if rejection were not a factor? What if there were *nothing* to fear? That's a very real possibility if you use the strategies described in this chapter.

To proceed, you'll need an open mind. Don't negate a partic-ular method just because it doesn't immediately appeal to you; conversely, don't assume that those that *do* initially appeal to you will work for everyone in your organization. It's all a matter of per-sonal preference, so review the information here from just one perspective—your own.

These strategies were developed by many different leaders who created ones that worked for them. Why, they figured, should any-one attempt to force-feed their preferred tactics to others merely because they worked for them? It can challenge a leader's ego to accept that no one has a lock on any strategy, and that there is no one-size-fits-all universally effective recruiting approach. This does not contradict the idea of duplication in terms of following a system such as The Five Step System mentioned earlier. I'm referring to *strategies and tactics* within a larger duplicable system or process for building your business.

This is why it is vital to give everyone in your organization the opportunity to select and employ their own favorite recruiting strategies. As previously explained, professional networkers engage daily in two primary activities: retailing and recruiting. This chapter focuses on the second.

To begin, realize this: Networkers, *not* prospects, cause rejection. It may surprise you to learn that rich networkers face virtually no rejection, whereas poor networkers can't seem to avoid it. This unfortunate reality is primarily the result of a general misunderstanding of what rejection actually *is*, and how and why it occurs. So before we begin our exploration of specific tools for rejection-free networking, we'll examine the phenomenon of rejection by defining it and understanding how networkers themselves—not prospects—cause it either by their *approach* or by their *internal response* to a prospect's decision.

UNDERSTANDING REJECTION

Rich networkers avoid what poor networkers create. Most human beings are hardwired to be skeptical and defensive. Like it or not, we humans share those traits. For that reason, people tend to become defensive when they're confronted by inappropriate questions or proclamations. This is why rejection is usually prompted by networkers who say the wrong thing to the wrong person in the wrong manner at the wrong time. It's also why avoiding rejection is a skill that must be learned.

Unfortunately, too many of us deny our role in rejection; therefore, it is also important to define denial to increase our understanding of the role it plays in networking. Denial is a self-imposed coping mechanism designed to protect the ego against information it can't or doesn't want to handle. Of course, nobody wants to believe that he or she has caused negative reactions in prospects. As bright entrepreneurs who *really care*, we think how dare those lucky prospects reject our efforts to help them escape the rat race? How could their rejection of us be *our* fault? How could prospects be so cruel and antagonistic? It only makes sense to deny our role in antagonizing those we are trying to help. Right? *Wrong.*

Here's what happens: Joe Newbie receives a one-size-fits-all, canned sales approach; or, worse, he makes one up that seems "okay." Examples:

> "Excuse me sir/ma'am, do you have all the money and time-freedom you want?"
>
> "Excuse me ma'am/sir, if I could show you a way to earn an extra $2,000 a month part-time from your home, would that interest you?"

Canned, one-size-fits-all sales approaches like these encourage—indeed, *demand*—a defensive response.

I've heard many of these approaches over the years, and I find them all to be equally pathetic. I don't know about you, but I am not about to admit to some total stranger on the street or in a mall that I'm broke and suffering through a stress-filled, miserable life. In fact, I may not even be willing to admit that to a psychotherapist during our first few sessions. People detest personal and inappropriate questions; that's why I said those approaches demand rejection. Who is willing to admit to a stranger, or even a friend, that he or she needs money? Really, any prospect who *doesn't* reject that kind of approach may be pathologically delusional.

Another version is the upline-tag-team-warm-market assault. ("Upline" refers to your team leader(s), often the person(s) who brought you into the business.) In this scenario, Joe Newbie is encouraged to make a list of his 10 best warm-market prospects so his upline can join him in what can only be described as a three-way prospect smackdown. I'm referring, of course, to a joint phone call in which the prospect is unaware that two people are about to bombard him or her.

Let's say that Joe gets his accountant on the phone, asks him some off-the-wall, inappropriate question about his finances, and before his accountant can politely deflect the advance, Joe introduces his upline sponsor, who proceeds to launch a full-blown inquisition. Like some Hulk Hogan perched on the top ropes, Joe's upline dives on top of the accountant and tries to pin him to the network marketing mat with canned answers, networking spin, and fake sincerity. In the end, the accountant may kindly reject the pitch, but he will not invite Joe to his Christmas party, ever again, and he will never join Joe's business. Worse, he'll warn all their mutual friends that Joe is trying to get everyone involved in a "pyramid scheme."

Rejection is an appropriate response to an inappropriate approach.

In contrast, when we approach people in a sane and intelligent manner, generally they will not reject us personally (unless they are sociopaths). They will, however, tend to react defensively when they feel accosted. This is a reality that rich networkers understand. While we certainly want to introduce the people we love most to our new business, we want to do so in a non-threatening manner. In many cases upline leaders need not be involved in the first call or if they are, it should be very low keyed, so as not to alienate your friends and family.

I can honestly say I haven't personally experienced rejection in two decades, nor have my veteran network associates. Have people told me they're not interested? Absolutely! But never once did they attack or reject me from a personal perspective.

THE REJECTION-FREE STRATEGIES

Rich networkers understand the power of numbers. Poor networkers focus on selling a handful of people, then attempt to manage them.

Keep in mind that there are numerous adult report cards—measures of success. It would be disingenuous of me to place maximum value on any one of them. Some people are motivated by money, others by titles. Some strive for celebrity, others for tenure. Some say that raising children properly is their ultimate priority, while others don't want children of their own because their careers mean everything to them. Some people are observers, others are doers. I respect everyone's choices. But for the purpose of this chapter I'm going to focus on the one reward that motivates most networkers: money. Most people enter this industry because they are interested in earning money. It would be untruthful to pretend otherwise.

There are those who may ignore our systems because they don't agree that money is important. Others may grow hostile and complain that we're too focused on worldly possessions. Sorry folks, but that's not the case. The purpose of this book is to help individuals achieve radical wealth once they've decided to succeed financially. Earning money is just one adult report card, but as I said, it is the candid focus of most entrepreneurs. Those who join our profession must understand this: network marketing is a numbers game. The more people you approach, the more you recruit; the more people you recruit, and the more products or services you sell, the more you earn. Period. End of the story.

It's not about "throwing a bunch of mud against the wall and hoping some of it sticks." Rather, it's about believing so fiercely in your product and opportunity that you honestly *want* to tell the world about your good fortune, and share the vehicle for achieving it with everyone who will listen. I've reviewed countless company pay plans, and none has a ceiling. If you want to earn $1 million a week, no one can stop you—except you. Again, the key is numbers. Rich networkers understand that this is a numbers game. Poor networkers don't seem to get it.

Certainly, some want recognition, and others are satisfied being able to make their car payment; still others just want to be part of a social network. That's fine. But if your motive is to create radical wealth, numbers are critical.

It's also important to realize that many in your team downline— the people who signed up in your organization beneath you—will not have the same goals as you. If you spend all your time supporting people who don't really care about building a huge organization, you will not achieve substantial financial goals in network marketing. It's not about right and wrong, smart or stupid. You must forgo the value judgments and simply do what it takes to make your dreams come true. More important, don't let "learners" sidetrack you by criticizing your motives.

Before I give you a numerical formula for success, I want to make certain you understand the distinction between "leaders" and "learners," because you will have both in your organization. A leader is someone who consistently demonstrates what's possible. A learner is someone who seeks information. The recruiting strategies I lay out next should appeal to both groups.

Rejection-Free Recruiting Strategy 1: The Lime-Green Card Advertisement

To implement this strategy, purchase a hundred or more lime-green 4-by-6 index cards. On the front, in black letters, have one of the following messages professionally printed in easy-to-read capital letters:

EARN $30K PER MONTH
WEAR DESIGNER CLOTHING
DRIVE A NEW MERCEDES
NOW INTERVIEWING
SERIOUS INQUIRIES ONLY [Your telephone number]

Many retail businesses hang bulletin boards where people can place business cards or ads. Your lime-green card will attract attention immediately, and your message will stimulate curiosity. Post those cards all over town and get ready for calls. (Note: While $30,000 to $50,000 per month will stimulate curiosity on the cards or bumper stickers, on billboards state a more reasonable amount, or people will drive past and ignore them. More on that in Rejection-Free Strategy 5.)

As follow-up, make sure that your voicemail message is very brief, friendly, and professional, telling callers you're currently unavailable. Ask them to leave their name and number, and tell them you'll call them back. Thank them for calling, and give them your sizzle call number (a short recorded call that creates intrigue and interest in checking out your business) and website address.

Do not record a sales message or mention your company or product on your voicemail. If you do, you'll lose half your prospects before they ever leave a name or number.

Rejection-Free Recruiting Strategy 2: Data-Specific Lists

A data-specific list is one of your greatest sources for prospects. By "data-specific," I mean a list on which are the names of people with whom you have things in common. They might be realtors, paraglide pilots, mountain climbers, or golfers; it doesn't really matter. What's so impressive about a data-specific list is that it allows you to build a huge warm market in a very short period of time.

One company that provides data-specific lists is SRDS, which you can find by going to www.srds.com. This company represents thousands of list brokers from all over the world. All you need to do is acquire a specific list of individuals who have something in common with you. If you find the cost prohibitive, form a team and share the costs and lists.

Here is a specific example of how I used data-specific recruiting, from a taped speech I made:

> I'm a paraglide pilot, and I acquired a list of paraglide pilots from the United States Hang Gliding Association. Once I got that list, I had immediate access to 30,000 people who paraglide in North America. The exciting fact is I had something in common with each of those people.

It's fairly simple to use data-specific lists: You just acquire one and then call the people on it, one at a time. Introduce yourself by pointing out that you do what they do. For example, I called paragliders and said, "Hello, my name is Mark Yarnell; I'm a paraglide pilot, and I understand that you are also." This created instant rapport every time I was able to reach a pilot. I next said, "This is going to sound crazy, but I think I have found a way for paraglide pilots like us to earn $30,000 to $50,000 a month and fly five days a week. Grab a pen and I'll give you a website link so you can check it out." In most cases, I didn't even ask them if the business would interest them. I just said something like, "Grab a pen, quick. I want to give you a link to a website where you can learn about what I'm up to!"

Data-specific lists are marvelous tools; they make it possible for individuals who have things in common—hobbies, professions, cultural interests, or sports, for example—to link with other like-minded people. Let's say you are a nurse, and you get a list of nurses who live and work within a thousand miles of your home. You call each of them, and identify yourself as a nurse. Then you point out that you have found a way for nurses to earn a whole lot of money. Ask them to grab a pen so that they can write down the contact information to check out what you're offering. That's how simple it is to use data-specific lists to prospect.

People have told me that they have absolutely no warm market; they claim to have no interests or hobbies, and not to belong to a church or any organizations, and so doubt they can create a list of people to become their prospects. But when I continue to ask them questions, eventually they find *something* they have in common with others. You, too, have huge potential markets that will respond favorably to your presentation once they realize you share similar interests. All you have to do is acquire lists and start calling; identify yourself and explain that you have found a way for "people like us" to earn significant money and spend more time doing what we love.

Other exciting—and underused—sources to tap for new prospects are employment agencies, recruiters, temp agencies, and headhunters. A young woman named Dionee from Knoxville, Tennessee, used this prospecting strategy, and in one year discovered a gold mine. Specifically, she found an employment agency in Knoxville and invited the owners, a couple, to lunch. She stated that she'd entered a new business and had an idea she wanted to bounce off them. Naturally, when faced with the opportunity to secure a new client, the pair agreed to meet her.

During lunch, Dionee made a very important inroad by asking one provocative question: Would the employment agency owners rather earn 5 percent of each of their client's monthly checks for life, or the normal fee equal to one month's income when they placed candidates in jobs. Put another way, would they be better off receiving a one-time commission check for placing a person in a job, or 5 percent of that person's income for life? You do the math.

Needless to say, this concept intrigued the couple. They responded that they would be much better off receiving a fee equal to 5 percent of the monthly checks of all those for whom they had found employment. That signaled the beginning of a mutually lucrative relationship between Dionee and the owners of the employment agency.

Dionee next placed the employment agency owners on her front line, and they set up interviews for her with job seekers in their database. The goal was to find personable, extroverted individuals, and interview them for sales positions that paid straight commissions. Dionee's agreement with the employment agency owners stipulated that the people she recruited would be placed on their front line, as well. In other words, she would personally recruit and sponsor these people so that the employment agency would benefit by getting a royalty on the sales of all who joined the organization.

Every city has employment agencies. Some are part of national chains, and are very difficult to work with in this way. Others, however, are locally owned, and these are the ones you want to approach. Again, it's as simple as letting the owners know that you have an idea that will make all of you a lot of money. Take them to lunch and offer them the opportunity to earn 5 or 10 percent per month on each person's check, versus a one-time fee. Watch their eyes light up.

Remember, employment agencies benefit tremendously whenever they place a person in a job. By forming an alliance with one of these agencies (which is the basis of Rejection-Free Recruiting Strategy 6), you develop a lifetime referral opportunity with individuals who are literally in business to obtain interviews for their clients. Additionally, you're building an organization headed by a professional who has a constant flow of new prospects, on a daily and weekly basis.

You only need one employment agency to staff a portion of your organization with very good salespeople. That strategic alliance alone will make you a great deal of money, because the agency is a rich source for effective prospecting and recruiting in network marketing.

Rejection-Free Recruiting Strategy 3: The Kiosk CD Handout

Do you realize that every mall in every city in North America has small booths, called kiosks, where people sell everything from cell phones to costume jewelry, candles, and food condiments? Many of those kiosks are managed by the people who lease them, not the clerks working at them for minimum wage. The key to the kiosk CD handout strategy is this: All you need to do is recruit one person who leases a kiosk in any mall.

That person will generally interact with many thousands of people every week, and even more on the weekends. They simply pick the ones who look responsible and friendly, and give them a free CD about your business. You enroll the kiosk manager on your front line, and agree that all the leads he or she generates will go directly under him or her, in order to build a power group.

The kiosk CD approach is absolutely marvelous! The number of potential prospects will be virtually limitless if you can recruit just three or four kiosk lessees in your community to assess consumers as they walk by, chat with those who seem responsible, and hand out CDs. Moreover, it's an effective way to filter through thousands of people on any given weekend in malls all over North America.

Additionally, some lessees will welcome your opportunity as a tremendous new cash flow source, which can only increase their productivity and profitability. Some will see the value in participating in this prospecting strategy, while others won't; regardless, you don't need many to prosper.

Approach these individuals with a simple question: "If you could earn an extra $10,000 per month right here, without any additional overhead, would it be worth it to you to go to lunch with me to learn how?"

Rejection-Free Recruiting Strategy 4: The Fate Approach

Laura Kall is one of the most brilliant young women in the history of network marketing, and her father, Richard Kall, is one of the best mentors anyone could ever have. When she first got out of college, Laura developed a strategy she called the "fate approach"—a tactic that comes fairly easily to an extrovert like Laura. The method worked as follows: Laura—who is from Long Island—would put herself in various places around Manhattan and Long Island where she would be surrounded by other people—such as standing in line at Grand Central Station, a movie theater, or a Broadway playhouse. Then, Laura would ask the man or woman standing closest to her if he or she believed in fate. Her goal was to strike up a conversation with professional-looking people who appeared a bit tired and burned out. Since that's the way most people are in today's business world, they were easy to find.

In response to Laura's question, people would generally say something like, "Well, what do you mean?" To which she would answer, "Do you believe that things happen for a reason? For example, here we are in a city of 10 million people. What are the odds that we would be standing in the same line at the same time? Of all the places in New York where we could have been right now among these millions of people, maybe fate has drawn us together." Then she would give them a CD, or a cassette tape, or a business card, and say, "I want you to think about it; I do believe in fate and I think we've been drawn together for a reason."

Laura told me that she acquired one of her best distributors in this manner as a result of a taxicab exchange. A man was getting out of a cab in front of the Plaza Hotel in Manhattan, and Laura could tell that he was fairly stressed out by the way he was rushing to pay the driver and grab hold of his briefcase. While he was still fumbling for cash to pay the driver, and Laura was waiting to get into the cab, she asked him if he believed in fate. The man said, "What are you talking about?" She answered, "Well, of all the cabs in New York City, how could we both have chosen this one? Here I am, a person who teaches men like you how to decompress, leave the rat race, and make a fortune from their homes, and here you are, obviously a mature and probably successful businessperson. What are the odds that, given all the cabs and taxi stands in New York City, I would just *happen* to be getting into the cab you're leaving? I believe in fate. Maybe we've been drawn together for a reason. I tell you what; let me give you this CD and you call me if it makes sense to you." Then she got into the cab and left.

When she got home, the man from the taxi, who by now had checked into the hotel, had gotten kind of interested in the whole idea of fate and decided to give her a call. They became friends. Eventually, he signed up, became a successful distributor on her front line, and the rest is history.

The fate approach is remarkably effective for those with the courage and the personality to be that forthright. It worked for Laura Kall. Why not try it yourself? Ask a few people you meet if they believe in fate. Chances are that by the time they get home they'll probably have started thinking about that question, and it'll nag at them until they give you a call to find out exactly why you asked it of them.

Rejection-Free Recruiting Strategy 5: The Billboard

I include this strategy because it's a wonderful way for a team of networkers to pool their money to generate a large number of prospect names, which they can then share. Admittedly, it's not an approach that most of you will take because of the cost. Billboards generally require a minimum of $800 to $1,000 per month. That means if 8 to 10 people in your organization agree to pitch in, you'll each be spending about $100 a month to put up a large billboard on a highway in a high-traffic area.

If you can afford to embark on this strategy, sit down with a group of people in your organization who also are willing to spend a little money on a high-traffic billboard and pool your resources. Just be sure you have a mechanism set up beforehand for sharing the leads when they come in.

The trick to this strategy is to keep the billboard message clean and simple. Remember, people will be driving—sometimes at high speed—past it, so it has to be brief, to the point, and easy to read. Two effective ideas are:

Exit the rat race forever. Earn $$$$ a month from home. [Phone number]
Hate this traffic? Work from home. Become wealthy. [Phone number]

Here's a simple question. While driving around your city over the last two or three years—or even in the last six months—have you noticed a billboard anywhere promoting a business opportunity? Chances are, you haven't. So why not capitalize on that gap?

There was a time when 8 to 12 of such billboard ads could be found on display in cities like Atlanta and Denver. Distributors at an insurance company posted some of them, and subsequently made millions of dollars; others were posted by distributors in big network marketing companies. Some of those distributors were members of a diet program promising customers they could lose weight in a hurry, and all they had to do was call the phone number listed. The ads were highly effective.

But here's what's important to understand about this prospecting strategy. Like so many others that work very effectively, it has been largely forgotten as more and more people have gone the cyberspace route. Everyone today seems to be fighting tooth and nail trying to figure out how to monetize website traffic. People all over the world are seeking ways to attract leaders through the Internet and other digital technologies. Sure, these high-speed tools are remarkable ways to transfer information, but they're not particularly effective for prospecting large numbers of people interested in a home business. And as the number of people using the Internet to prospect grows, many of the more traditional, down-to-earth techniques, which are still effective, are being abandoned.

Today, there are very few, if any, billboards in the United States that inspire people to investigate how they can earn radical income or have more free time. Now that you know you can advertise for $800 to $1,000 a month, why not take advantage of this wide-open opportunity? Pull together a group of people in your organization and raise the capital to post a billboard. By doing so, you will garner an unlimited number of leads to share with one another.

Make certain that the billboard copy states that you're looking for people who are interested in earning big money. One word of caution in this regard: Tone down the income potential. Amounts in the $10,000 to $15,000 a month range will grab people's attention. If, on the other hand, you advertise incomes over $15,000 a month on a billboard, the average person will drive right past and ignore it, because they can't relate to it. Keep your numbers exciting but realistic. Also, regulators tend to take action only against those that make, or even imply, an unrealistic earnings claim, so don't suggest that you are earning a huge amount.

In summary, the billboard is a great way to attract large numbers of people, if you can lease one for several months in a high-traffic area.

Rejection-Free Recruiting Strategy 6: The Job Fair

Did you know that dozens of job fairs are held all year long in cities all over North America? If you're thinking of attending one of these as a source of prospects, your goal should not be to purchase a booth and pay money for the privilege of having people mill past it. What makes better sense is to take a stack of CDs related to your specific company, pay your entrance fee to the fair, and then set out to meet as many people as you can, handing out the CDs as you go.

A recent job fair in my area was attended by an estimated 38,000 people. That's 38,000 people who were considering a job change. If you can describe a better environment for recruiting people than one where they are looking for work, I would like to know what it is. As I said, there are job fairs everywhere, and it is most definitely worth making the trip to any nearby community to attend one. At every job fair in every community you'll find thousands upon thousands of weary job hunters wandering around looking for solutions to their financial difficulties. I know people in network marketing who create entire databases of leads simply by walking around job fairs and meeting individuals.

I have been told, however, that some networkers feel "funny" about recruiting at job fairs, because they are not paying for a booth, suggesting that it seems unethical. I disagree. There are two things important to keep in mind about job fairs. One is that there are a number of companies at them offering salaried positions and jobs of various kinds. Two, thousands of people are wandering around hoping to find a better alternative to their current employment situation. It really doesn't matter whether you're in a booth handing out information or a member of the crowd handing out information. Both methods of reaching out at job fairs are ethical.

The rejection-free prospecting technique that works best at a job fair is, simply, to meet people, get their cards, and call them later. Do not walk around introducing yourself to people or giving out *your* business card. Do not leave brochures laying around in restrooms and other public areas at the job fair.

I know one distributor from Denver who went all the way to San Diego to participate in what was billed as a huge job fair. He came home with hundreds of prospect names. Another gentleman went to Las Vegas to attend a technology fair that had nothing to do with job acquisitions. He came home with over 500 business cards after only two days of wandering around, wearing a button that read, "My company is looking for three good people." The moral: Don't miss out on job fairs! They are gold mines filled with network marketing opportunities.

Rejection-Free Recruiting Strategy 7: The Pall Bearer

I've saved the million-dollar rejection-free recruiting strategy for the very last. Pay attention, because this one is going to save you from having to compete with masses of people in this industry. I call it the *pall bearer strategy* for this reason: It requires you to contact every person who becomes your prospect every six months until that person either signs up in your organization, or you become a pall bearer at his or her funeral.

You must track your contacts assiduously to reap the rewards of this strategy. You can do so either by purchasing appropriate tracking software, or by taking this much less complex approach:

1. Get a recipe box that holds 4 × 6 index cards, and insert dividers for January through December. Now you have 12 sectional dividers in your card file.
2. Insert 30 blank cards, numbered 1 through 30, behind every divider.
3. Whenever you talk to people about your business (assuming that they're pleasant), fill out a card on each of them. Include their contact information, along with anything that will help jog your memory about them.
4. Insert the completed card behind the divider that is exactly six months from today in your card file.

Here's why this is so important: The average networker, if not the majority of them, pitch away prospects as if they were disposable.

Here's a statistic to keep in mind: People change jobs in North America about every 3.7 years. The key is to catch them in one of those change windows; when you do, they can become partners for life. The reason I call number 7 the most important rejection-free strategy is this: After you've talked to a prospect one time, that person will not reject you—*if* you approach him or her properly in half a year.

Stay in touch with everyone. If you contact prospects about your business and they join, great. If they say no, put them in your card file behind the divider six months from the day you call. Why? Because when you get out of bed on, say, January 16, you'll have 28 people to call that you spoke with six months ago to the day.

And here's how to make these calls rejection-free—it's a very simple process: Let's say you talk to Bob today, and he isn't interested. Simply say, "May I check back with you in half a year, just to see if anything in your life has changed?" Bob will generally be pleasant (and amenable to ending the call quickly), so he will likely reply, "Certainly, the time is not right now, but call me again if you like."

When you call Bob six months later, along with the other 25 to 30 people in your card file for that day, approach him in the following way: "Hi, Bob, it's Mark Yarnell. We haven't talked for half a year, but you told me I could check back with you in six months or so. I'm giving you a call to see if you can use that extra $30,000 a month now. Just to jog your memory, when we talked six months ago, you indicated you didn't need an extra $30,000 to $50,000 a month. I'm just calling you to see if anything in your life has changed since then, and if you could use that extra cash now." If Bob says no again, boom: put his card six months ahead in your card file and call him again then.

Remember, the pall bearer recruiting strategy is called that to remind you *never to give up* on prospects. Contact them every six months until they sign up or die.

The vast majority of networkers call a prospect only one time and then discard that person's name, as if they were throwaways. They then go out and start looking for *new* prospects. *Never* throw prospects names away, as ultimately you may catch them in a change window. They've been downsized or outsourced; they hate their boss; or they've lost their revenue stream—whatever the reason, they very well might want to hear from you the next time you call. When you check with people every six months, and treat them right, eventually you're going to catch some of them at exactly the right time.

Perseverance and timing, together, are the hallmarks of the pall bearer recruiting strategy. Remember this above all else: Make a card for every single prospect. Include their names and numbers on it, plus any references to previous conversations. Always place their cards in your file six months ahead to the day you last spoke to them. Eventually, you'll catch them at the right time and right place in their life, and they'll be willing to consider your business as a solution. What a marvelous idea!

There you have it—seven rejection-free strategies for recruiting. Virtually every personality type is represented in them, so you should be able to choose at least a couple that feel right to you. And that, of course, is the key, because the odds of everyone in an entire downline sharing the same personality traits, skills, and interests are zero. That is why one-size-fits-all canned scripts *don't work*. While a duplication system may seem ideal at first, it soon causes frustration for those who are uncomfortable using it. And once they become frustrated, and don't have options for growing their contact list, they will quit the business.

In closing, I want to remind you that fear of rejection is the hobgoblin of new independent business owners. Use the seven strategies in this chapter and conquer that fear. No more fear; no more rejection.

BUILDING THE ULTIMATE FAMILY LEGACY

Shelby Hall

I could've "had a V8!"

Do you remember that old commercial, in which a man slaps his forehead as he remembers all he had to do was drink one can of V8 juice, instead of eating a bunch of vegetables he didn't like? Many of us can relate to that commercial, albeit in a somewhat different way. We wonder what we have to show for working hard all our lives. What are the lasting results of our labor? Many of us believed we could provide a better life for our children than we had. How did we do? Will we leave a legacy that our kids will be proud of?

My husband was born in England and arrived in the United States in 1960. From the moment he arrived, he couldn't wait until the day he could call himself an American. He worked hard for seven years before he earned his U.S. citizenship. He had to become familiar with the U.S. *Constitution* and its amendments, and learn U.S. history, in particular leading up to America's independence from Great Britain. He has told me often that he found studying that period in American history quite humorous, given that the accounts of the American War of Independence were much different from those he had read growing up in England.

My husband has been a citizen now for 44 years and feels every bit as American as those who were born here. At the same time, he is proud of the legacy he inherited from the land where he was born; it has remained with him, and will throughout his life. We have worked hard to educate our four children about that heritage, and have made a point of taking them to England to walk the lanes and cobblestone streets of the tiny coal mining village where their father spent his early years. That kind of legacy is priceless.

Legacies need not be related to valuable assets, toys, or wealth in any way. *Webster's Dictionary* defines legacy as, "a gift by will, especially of money or other personal property; something transmitted by or received from an ancestor or predecessor or from the past." An American legacy might be one of religious freedom, or the free enterprise system that is a hallmark of the U.S. economy and forms the core of a capitalistic and free market society.

Sometimes, however, legacy does stem from personal wealth. My father-in-law ("Dad") died at age 85 in August 2009. He was a coal miner who wanted more for his wife and children, and so in May of 1960 he uprooted his entire family from their home in England and moved them to the United States. My husband, who was 15 years old at the time, remembers it well.

Even though my father-in-law had always worked as a coal miner, after he left England, he was forced to do something else—and that something else was just about anything he could do to earn enough to support his family. They didn't have much, but they didn't care; they were in America now, and they knew the lean times would soon pass.

Dad made extraordinary strides in the years following his arrival in America. When he retired at age 62, he was a director at the Clark County Housing Authority in Las Vegas, Nevada—not bad for an old coal miner with only an eighth-grade education. He wanted what he needed, and he wanted it badly—so he did whatever he had to do to make it happen. Dad's story is not unique in this country; countless others have come to America for the chance to participate in its free market economy, which allows anyone to succeed if they apply themselves and work hard.

Six weeks before he died, Dad presented my husband with a chronological history of his life, which he had written over a 20-year period. Some of it he had typed on an old typewriter; other parts he had written in long hand; and toward the end, he used a computer. The hard-copy segments comprised 225 single-spaced pages with quarter-inch margins, headers, and footers. Dad asked my husband to organize his words without changing them, and to arrange them into a format that would be easy for everyone—especially for his children, grandchildren, and generations to come—to read.

This daunting task took my husband more than a year to complete. He enhanced his father's story by adding appropriate photographs of relatives, people, places, and special events, to make it come alive and be more enjoyable. The result is nothing short of amazing. The finished book of 245,000 words is contained in 18 chapters, totaling 630 pages and 501 photos and illustrations. It has been leather-bound and distributed to the entire extended family.

My husband is now writing his own life story. He knows he has much to be thankful for, and feels strongly that he too must record his history for our children and the generations that will follow us.

There's a simple lesson here: Be sure to set up your new networking business with your family in mind. Obtain legal counsel so that you can protect your financial legacy as part of your will, and to limit the tax burden and other liabilities that could interfere with or diminish your legacy.

During recessionary times like these, people can get hurt in a volatile market; some end up using their IRAs like ATM machines. Some saved for this rainy day by hiding their profits under the mattress. We thought we were invincible when we were young, and convinced ourselves that we had plenty of time to build a nest egg for our later years. We all planned to invest, but at some time "in the future." Suddenly, the future is here, and we're smacking ourselves on the forehead, saying, "I could've had a V8."

Gone is the time when that type of thinking will work for us. No longer is even the time-tested security of home equity a slam-dunk. Pensions from the companies many of us worked at for 40 years have all but disappeared—or have been drastically reduced. And unless you are a seasoned investor, the stock market is no longer a secure place to park large sums of money. A 401K can become a 201K overnight, so we have to be vigilant in managing those funds.

Real estate was traditionally considered the "safe place" to invest. The saying was that "God's not making any more dirt," the implication being that land values would always increase. Though it's still true that God will not be making more dirt, the return on real estate investments has become a long-term play.

Any savvy financial counselor will tell you that the best insurance for financial security in your later years is to create some passive and residual income while you are still young enough and able. Network marketing has proven to be just such a vehicle for people like you and me, enabling us to generate sufficient residual income to give us financial security well into our retirement years, with the added advantage that we can leave it to our heirs.

Even some who waited too long to build a nest egg, and arrived at retirement without enough in reserve, have found network marketing an ideal source of continued income. The greatest benefit of this industry is that it enables us to live a good life and remain vital and productive as long as we desire. Along the way, we can develop meaningful relationships with hundreds, and possibly thousands, of people we consider the "warm market" for our new network marketing opportunity.

The beauty of this model is that you can dedicate the first two or three years of your retirement—while you are still reasonably fresh and energetic—to building your new business. Thereafter, you can begin to coast, and allow those people you brought in below you in your organization to begin to carry the load of maintenance and expansion.

Although certainly there are exceptions, I doubt that many people truly want to be couch potatoes, or be forced to clip coupons in their later years to make ends meet. I believe that most feel they still have a lot to offer. On the other hand, they also don't want to work so hard anymore. My husband's definition of "real retirement" is doing what you want to do when you want to do it. And a second career in network marketing will allow you to do just that.

I ask you now to think about what happened to your dreams of the past? Are you willing to let them just fade away, or are you ready to make them a reality? You might worry that you're too old to start a new career. After all, you've worked for 40-plus years, raised a family, taken some wonderful vacations, and are pretty sure you can exist on your savings and the subsidy from your Social Security check.

Enough of that nonsense! Who in the world wants to just *exist*? You are wiser and more experienced now than at any other time in your life; are you really planning to park all that hard-earned knowledge on the sidelines? I don't think so. Remember, age is just a number, nothing more.

When my husband asked my opinion about beginning a new company at age 63, my response was: "How old will you be if you *don't* start this new company?" In other words, starting over has nothing to do with age; it has to do with desire and drive. Harland Sanders started the Kentucky Fried Chicken company when he was 65 years old; even now, long after his passing at age 90, his legacy is strong; his image is seen in thousands of restaurants around the world. His legacy was extended further by Dave Thomas, an early partner of Sanders and, later, founder of Wendy's Old-Fashioned Hamburgers, another global fast-food giant.

I add Larry H. Miller to this list. Larry grew up in Utah, and although he didn't receive much of a formal education, he had a keen sense of how to make a dollar. He also had a passion for cars, and soon became owner of one dealership, then two, and then several. In the 1980s, Larry purchased an NBA team, the New Orleans Jazz, and moved it to Utah. As a Utah Jazz fan myself, I've long noticed Larry sitting in his usual seat on the front row of the arena, cheering on his favorite team. Still later, he built the Larry H. Miller Motorsports Park, which serves nowadays as the venue for countless world-class auto-racing events.

Larry also involved his family in his businesses, and encouraged them to take part and enjoy what they were building together. His children witnessed their parents making huge contributions to the community, both via their considerable influence and their financial generosity. Larry has passed away but his son Greg is now running Miller Enterprises, following the lessons he learned from his father throughout the years. They appear to be a close family; and though very busy, they always put family values at the core of their various interests.

Henry Ford is another of my favorite industrialists. I find it humorous that at one point in his life he wanted to liquidate his entire entities, one at a time, and convert those assets into cash. His wife put a stop to that, telling him, in no uncertain terms, that it was *not* going to happen. Mrs. Ford wanted everything left to the family, so that her kids and grandkids could one day benefit from the legacy of a great company, rather than be left with bank accounts full of cash. And that is precisely what happened; even today, Ford's descendants are involved in the many moving parts of Ford Enterprises.

These stories, obviously, are not all directly related to the network marketing industry; but they do all serve as great examples of entrepreneurs who have built and left legacies for their families and communities.

One story I love that is related to network marketing is that of Judge Vernon Douglas, a man who has served as the chief circuit judge of the Florida Third Judicial Court since 2007. Judge Douglas was admitted to the Florida Bar in 1973, after earning his law degree from Stetson University. His twin brother Marshall began a career in accounting, and at some point became aware—by way of the income tax filings he was doing for his clients who were successful at their networking businesses—of the money he himself could make in network marketing. Twenty years ago, he began his own networking career, yet he was never able to convince his younger brother, the judge, to join him.

Then, in 2009, Marshall joined a new start-up network marketing company, which held great prospects for him. He hoped that it would also open the door for him and Vernon to work together; he saw it as the perfect opportunity to once again try to convince his brother to give network marketing a chance. This time, it worked.

Vernon began to work at his newfound networking business, even as he maintained his judgeship. He was so pleased by his early success as a networker that he soon began to think about committing all of his time to the venture. To that end, he decided he needed a plan that would enable him to retire from the bench much sooner than he had originally planned. His goal was simple: As soon as his networking business generated the same amount of money he was making as a judge, he would schedule his retirement from the bench. Only 10 months later, he did so.

Judge Douglas's experience is not unusual; it actually happens all the time in this business. He will leave a wonderful reputation and legacy as a Florida State judge; at the same time, he now has enough residual income to allow him to enjoy the years to come and secure his legacy to his heirs.

Let's agree right now that you are *not* going to have the regrets of so many individuals toward the end of their careers. It's time to show those regrets the door and get on with the life you planned—and *deserve*.

Network marketing will allow you to have experiences you never could otherwise. As your income increases, the time you need to work will diminish—and you will find yourself with enough time to do more of what you always wanted to do but could never squeeze in between your countless responsibilities. You will also be able to travel more, and spend more quality time with your family and friends.

I've always thought that the path most people take in life is somewhat backward. We are born, we grow, and in the early stages of life we develop our personal skills. We somehow survive our teenage years, get through college and our first jobs, and then find ourselves married with children. For the next 20 years all we can focus on is how to pay the mortgage on time and give the kids a decent upbringing and a good education. We become so fixated on being effective wage earners that we miss out on much of what we want so desperately—family time. Then, before we know it, the kids are grown and have their own children, and we are alone again. The period of your life when you have the most resources is when your child-rearing years are behind you—but in the words of country singer Kenny Chesney's hit ballad Don't Blink, "we blinked" and missed a lot along the way.

Since becoming associated with the network marketing business, my husband and I spend more time together than at any other period in our lives. We've been empty-nesters for about 13 years, and have put those years to good use by investing our time in our networking business. Needless to say, we are also enjoying life more and getting to know one another once again. After all, we were married, had children right away, then spent 30 plus years raising them, and we never really had time together until after they left home. I think this is an experience a lot of you can relate to.

Now, he and I want to work together as a couple. I don't want to be one of those wives who follows her husband around the local hardware store. I want to be "fully loaded" with the information I need to make the decision on whether we need a PVC connector or an elbow to fix the sprinkling system. This means I walk alongside him, not behind him. The empowerment you gain from working alongside your partner when you own your own network marketing home-based business is truly thrilling—especially when you know you are doing it for the right reasons. You enjoy knowing that you are working for your family, and that you are doing right by others, as well as for yourself. It is vital to your peace of mind that you give others the opportunity to be as successful as you are. But perhaps the greatest benefit of owning your own network marketing business is the feeling of independence and self-reliance inherent in this business model. It is liberating to know that you own your own business, and that you cannot be laid off, unless you want to be. You have the power to excel at top speed or at a slower pace that's more comfortable for you. There is no one breathing down your neck, pushing you to work harder. No longer do you have to worry about whether government entitlements will survive the next round of budget cuts, or the stock market will wipe out your 401K.

The business of network marketing allows you to head a team composed of good leaders, who, like you, are self-starters eager to achieve liberation. Together, you can create a powerful and enduring team, which in time will provide lasting security for all of you.

Network marketing cannot, in and of itself, create a legacy for you. What it can do is provide the vehicle in which you can travel to the destination of your dreams.

ABOUT THE AUTHORS

Mark Yarnell is the author of 11 books, including the international best-seller *Your First Year in Network Marketing*. As a network marketing leader, he has built an organization of 300,000 people in 21 countries.

Along with Dr. Charles King of Harvard University, Mark created the first certification course in network marketing, which has been taught at the University of Illinois, Chicago, and in Seoul, Korea, since 1993.

Mark was named Philanthropist of the Year by the *Washington Times*, honored with The American Dream Award from The Howard

Ruff Company, named The Greatest Networker in the World by *Upline*, and inducted into the Network Marketing Hall of Fame.

Valerie Bates has over 25 years of business experience; she has enjoyed successful careers in teaching, management consulting, and network marketing. But it is thanks to network marketing that Valerie was able to be a work-from-home mom when her children were young.

Prior to reengaging in network marketing 10 years ago, Valerie owned a management consulting practice, where she conducted strategic planning, business planning, and conflict resolution for corporations, government organizations, and not-for-profit entities in Canada and the United States. She also designed and taught numerous programs on leadership, change, facilitation, and personal development.

Valerie is the author of four network marketing and personal development books.

Today, Valerie and Mark Yarnell are actively building their networking business. Their goal is to help others rise to their full potential and enjoy greater freedom and fulfillment. Married 10 years ago, the couple lives in beautiful British Columbia, surrounded by mountains, lakes, and best of all, family.

Derek Hall is an industry veteran of 44 years, who says he has flunked retirement three times. He has created corporate cultures that put the success of distributors and employees first. He's a steadfast believer in the concept of servant leadership, which emphasizes the CEO's role as steward of a company's resources. By remaining focused on fiscal responsibility and managed growth, he ensures that companies will be profitable, sustainable, and scalable.

Derek knows what it means to seek a better life. As a 15-year-old, he emigrated from England to America, when his father, who had worked in the Yorkshire coal mines for 21 years, decided he didn't want his two sons to follow in his footsteps.

Derek began his career as a truck driver at a Fortune 500 company and eventually worked his way up the ranks to become chief sales officer of what was then an $11 billion company. This profound life experience convinced him that with determination and hard work unbounded personal success was possible. Derek went on to serve as CEO for four other companies. It was at one of these where he fell in love with the network marketing distribution model.

At age 64, and still feeling he had much more to give, with four partners he created a new network marketing company and incorporated into it all he had learned in his previous years in business.

Derek has been married to his wife, Shelby, for 44 years. They have 4 children and 18 grandchildren and are enjoying their new adventure together.

Shelby Hall was born in Ogden, Utah, and is a graduate of Weber State University. She left her position at the IRS to begin a family. Since then she has held the distinguished roles of wife and mother of 4 children; and for the past 20 years, she has excelled as a grandmother.

During the 1970s, while her husband was an executive in the pharmaceutical industry, she was elected president of the ladies auxiliary of the Utah Pharmaceutical Association and served on the Salt Lake City Council of Women. Shelby has also served as PTA president, taught seminary classes, and been involved in a variety of community endeavors; she has long been an active member of her church.

Shelby also has been involved, both directly and vicariously, with her husband Derek in the companies he has created and led. She becomes passionate about the products sold by these companies, and the people working within them, so it's no wonder that Derek introduces her as the chairman of the board.

More recently, since becoming an "empty nester" Shelby has travelled far and wide with Derek; she frequently shares the stage with him, and expresses her excitement and enthusiasm for their latest business adventure.

Shelby and Derek live in St. George, Utah, in the heart of Redrock Country, and are enjoying their many adventures together.

INDEX